The Writer's Runway

Volume 1

Info, Insights, & Affirmations

100 Strategies
for the
Aspiring Writer's Head, Heart, & Soul.

By
Danae Andrea Harwood

ISBN: 1502383403
ISBN-13: 978-1502383402

Printed by CreateSpace
Available from Amazon.com and other retail outlets.
Kindle version available.

Dedication

I dedicate this book to my son-beams, Sabre and Jaeger, to my lionhearted husband, Jim, and to Mum who embraces all. I cherish your love and support. You help me see in the dark and celebrate in the light.

I thank Yiayia and the fabulous Fountis Family for all their help and *agapi* over the years.

I have written this book in loving memory of our poet, Pappou, who passed over on 15th July 2013. He was a passionate, kind man and a fellow writer with aspirations.

CONTENTS

	Preface	xi
~ Insight 1 ~	Open	1
~ Insight 2 ~	I Am a Writer	3
~ Insight 3 ~	Words Count	4
~ Insight 4 ~	Come What May	6
~ Insight 5 ~	Other Ways to Count	8
~ Insight 6 ~	Explore	10
~ Insight 7 ~	The Visible Workout	12
~ Insight 8 ~	The Invisible Workout	14
~ Insight 9 ~	Alternative Routes to Success	15
~ Insight 10 ~	Please My Higher Self	17
~ Insight 11 ~	Nurture Talent and Hone Skills	18
~ Insight 12 ~	Write For the Right Reasons	20
~ Insight 13 ~	The Yellow Brick Roads	22
~ Insight 14 ~	Build Up Knowledge	25
~ Insight 15 ~	Belief Power	27
~ Insight 16 ~	The Alpha and the Omega	29
~ Insight 17 ~	Score Goals	31
~ Insight 18 ~	Respond Rather Than React	33
~ Insight 19 ~	Build Up a Calendar	34
~ Insight 20 ~	Success Appeal	36

CONTENTS CONTINUED

~ Insight 21 ~	Reject Rejection	38
~ Insight 22 ~	Embrace Technology and Change	40
~ Insight 23 ~	The Best Policy	41
~ Insight 24 ~	Juggle and Balance	43
~ Insight 25 ~	Invite Lord Maitreya	44
~ Insight 26 ~	From Topic to Toe	46
~ Insight 27 ~	Keep a Lookout	48
~ Insight 28 ~	Competition	49
~ Insight 29 ~	Build a Wonder of the World	51
~ Insight 30 ~	What If?	53
~ Insight 31 ~	Fill Up	55
~ Insight 32 ~	Lateral Thinking	57
~ Insight 33 ~	Shed Some Gravity	59
~ Insight 34 ~	Hop Around on Lily Pads	60
~ Insight 35 ~	Fix the Wonky Wheel	62
~ Insight 36 ~	New Angles on Old Ideas	63
~ Insight 37 ~	Jump Off the Band Wagon	66
~ Insight 38 ~	L.U.C.K. - Labour Under Correct Knowledge	68
~ Insight 39 ~	Pre-planned Plots	70
~ Insight 40 ~	Family and Friends Follow My Lead	72
~ Insight 41 ~	Act Up	73

CONTENTS CONTINUED

~ Insight 42 ~   Escape and Survival   76

~ Insight 43 ~   Plot Trees   78

~ Insight 44 ~   Duty of Care to Characters   80

~ Insight 45 ~   Draw the Lines   82

~ Insight 46 ~   Write in the Dark   83

~ Insight 47 ~   Go to the Inner Sanctuary   85

~ Insight 48 ~   Get Down   87

~ Insight 49 ~   Heed the Rules   90

~ Insight 50 ~   Get On With It   92

~ Insight 51 ~   Character Cards   94

~ Insight 52 ~   Hold Onto the Dream   96

~ Insight 53 ~   Done and Dusted   98

~ Insight 54 ~   What's It Worth?   100

~ Insight 55 ~   Invite Paul the Venetian Master   101

~ Insight 56 ~   Basic Instructions for a Sweet Ride   103

~ Insight 57 ~   Network with an Open Heart   104

~ Insight 58 ~   Put On a Show   106

~ Insight 59 ~   Chances Are   108

~ Insight 60 ~   How to Tell   109

~ Insight 61 ~   Purge the Passive   111

~ Insight 62 ~   Send the Strongest Signals   113

CONTENTS CONTINUED

~ Insight 63 ~   Write in Multi-dimensional Form   115

~ Insight 64 ~   Where's the Draft Coming From?   117

~ Insight 65 ~   The Business of Business   119

~ Insight 66 ~   Plagiarism Beats Obscurity   121

~ Insight 67 ~   Be a Dream Catcher   123

~ Insight 68 ~   Be a Thought Watcher   125

~ Insight 69 ~   First Impressions – the Basics   126

~ Insight 70 ~   Fear Less   128

~ Insight 71 ~   Make More Senses   130

~ Insight 72 ~   Write to the Tune   132

~ Insight 73 ~   Be Adjustable   133

~ Insight 74 ~   Set Off the Fireworks   135

~ Insight 75 ~   My Creative Space   137

~ Insight 76 ~   Write In the Zone   139

~ Insight 77 ~   Invite Master Lady Nada   140

~ Insight 78 ~   Humility   142

~ Insight 79 ~   Give and Receive   144

~ Insight 80 ~   Step Into the Pro's Life Daily   145

~ Insight 81 ~   Be an Attitude Athlete   147

~ Insight 82 ~   Works in Progress   149

~ Insight 83 ~   Entitled   151

CONTENTS CONTINUED

~ Insight 84 ~	I Am a Co-Creator	153
~ Insight 85 ~	Tough Love	154
~ Insight 86 ~	Forgive and Forgiven	156
~ Insight 87 ~	Consistency is King	157
~ Insight 88 ~	Learn From Successful Writers	159
~ Insight 89 ~	The Magic Never Leaves	161
~ Insight 90 ~	Advocate	163
~ Insight 91 ~	Introvert	164
~ Insight 92 ~	Along the Writer's Journey	166
~ Insight 93 ~	First Impressions Count with Characters	168
~ Insight 94 ~	Employ the Decoy	170
~ Insight 95 ~	Boys and Girls Come Out to Play	171
~ Insight 96 ~	Invite Master Sanat Kumara	173
~ Insight 97 ~	Box of Tricks	174
~ Insight 98 ~	Intersperse Duties	177
~ Insight 99 ~	All Writing Benefits Me	179
~ Insight 100 ~	Hand It Over	181
References		183
About the Author		186
Disclaimer		188

~ Preface ~

If you're a writer with strong career dreams, *The Writer's Runway* is for you. From the author's experience as a writer with aspirations, the best approach to long term writing is to have a holistic view that supports the head, heart, and soul. There are two well-known maxims: *the key to life is balance* and *happiness is the meaning and purpose of life.* It follows that the writer's whole self needs to be nurtured and protected to help facilitate a happy, balanced writing life filled with purpose, achievement, and financial reward.

The Writer's Runway aims to provide a source of balance that promotes fulfilment and longevity as a writer. This book consists of one hundred writing strategies and is a collation of reliable information, honest insights, and affirmations. The author wants to share these strategies with you because they have helped her along the writing journey and continue to do so.

Pursuing the dream to become a commercially viable writer can be challenging. Writing is generally a solitary activity. Writers need to persist in order to achieve their goals. The knowledge to gain about writing can seem endless and learning how to improve is an ongoing process. Lots can happen beneath the writer's surface and it's a healthier approach to share and validate these feelings along the way.

The Writer's Runway is your companion and confidante. It's a guide that imparts to you more than facts and practical tips. The book relays many of the experiences you may have on the writing journey to your dream destination and brings to the fore thoughts and feelings that could assist you with your own. *The Writer's Runway* also suggests self-talk to help keep you moving forwards on an even keel.

Info. Insights. Affirmations.

The book's three communication modes aim to strengthen your writing mind, body, and spirit in preparation for your launch into the marketplace. The book leans more towards fiction writers, but a lot of information and suggestions apply to writing in general so every reader stands to benefit.

The Info: *The Writer's Runway* consists of practical writing tips that the author has gathered from various sources and regards as valuable. The information includes suggestions on how to work towards a quality end product, checklists, how to find golden ideas, ways to approach different writing tasks and challenges, and facts about the industry.

The Insights: *The Writer's Runway* offers the author's observations on topics such as staying on the writing path, dealing with the double-edged sword called attitude, and relating to loved ones as a writer. The saying *there's a fine line between pleasure and pain* can sometimes apply to writing, however the author believes that your perspective and approach can help you choose and control the way you feel about it. Also, this book may relate to you when the 'non-writers' in your life are unable to and you need to feel understood.

The Affirmations: These help to build and fortify your belief system about writing, your dreams, and your capabilities. The affirmations serve to encapsulate the info and insights by putting them in a way that you may repeat and internalise. This can be likened to talking to your higher self and conditioning your subconscious to think the way you'd like it to about writing.

Important Notes

1)   It takes time to absorb the good information available to you from various sources and to develop the craft of writing for marketplace success. Therefore, patience and persistence are paramount to achieving your writing dreams.

New information needs time to carve grooves into your mind. With each reading the new information becomes more ingrained, enabling you to begin incorporating it into your actions.

Practising what you learn on a regular basis helps to dig even deeper channels in your writer's landscape to the point that the information becomes an established natural part of your topography. With application, knowledge can become a sense of knowing rather than data that you may need to recall and use somewhat mechanically.

2)   There are four insights that refer to Ascended Masters. The author's intention for these is simply to encourage inspiration and the feeling of greatness in order to help you create a mindset conducive to writing, as opposed to them being a promotion of any spiritual ideology.

You might prefer to adjust these passages and substitute the Ascended Masters with masters or muses of your choice such as other writers or heroes, alternative spiritual figures, your higher self, an inspiring organisation, or anything you create that represents inspiration, peace, and attainment to you and helps to bring your mind and emotions to the state that you desire in preparation for writing.

3)   The author has written this book in Australian (UK) English and so you may find some spelling variations such as colour rather than color, traveller instead of traveler, mum rather than mom, fantasise instead of fantasize, and so on.

4)   This book is in first person with the aim of helping you make the information, insights, and affirmations your own.

Ways to Use this Book

Preferably read one strategy per day. Re-visit each insight to help you consolidate your learning and renew your assurance. You may choose to read each topic in sequence. Or you could allow your intuition to guide you by letting the book fall open to the message that you might need to read at that point in time.

Conclusion

As a writer with career aspirations you've chosen a road that requires physical, mental, and spiritual workouts along the way specific to the writing journey. You're more likely to be a happy traveller, last the distance, and reach your destination if you are fit and strong in these three personal aspects. This brave, honest book aims to provide you with support as a trusty travelling companion, guide, and confidante.

Good luck with your writing endeavours. May you write onwards and upwards and accomplish all that you set out to do.

Best wishes,

Danae

~ Insight 1 ~

Open

I open *The Writer's Runway* with my mind open to receive its contents. I welcome the information, support, and understanding this book offers. I invite the book's messages to accompany me on my writing journey so they may enhance the experience and help keep my aspirations airborne.

I allow reliable advice and information from all sources to permeate my thinking and help me advance towards my writing dreams. I listen to unfamiliar information with open ears and pan for the gold in them. I re-read familiar information to reinforce what I've learned and absorb more from it. I consider ideas and suggestions that may seem strange or daunting at first. I'm open to accept truths about myself, my writing, and the industry.

I'm excited about making improvements by internalising information and putting what I learn into practice. However, I refrain from expecting myself to absorb and apply everything I learn immediately for this is an unrealistic approach. The assimilation of knowledge requires time and training.

Writing information can seem endless and at times this may feel overwhelming. Employing the knowledge I've gained can feel awkward and unnatural. Sometimes I might feel that achieving writing excellence, or writing a profitable book, or becoming a successful career writer is perhaps out of reach. All these feelings are normal. All writers feel unsure at points along the writing journey, but the writers who succeed are the ones who keep going and remain open to the possibilities.

Affirmation

My mind is open to the information from this book and other sources. I'm open to improving and applying the knowledge I gain step by step over time. I'm confident that whatever I learn will fall into place if I use it and remain patient. I'm open to exploring myself and writing. The possibilities that lie ahead are open ended. I remain open to the joys of writing at every stage of my development. My openness is the first gateway to my success.

~ Insight 2 ~

I Am a Writer

Let's get something straight. I'm the type of aspiring writer who has goals to achieve rather than the type who aspires to write some day. Writing is part of who I am and I embrace it here and now.

I write to feel satisfied and complete. I have the need to convey thoughts, feelings, information, and observations in text form. I express myself best and most comfortably via the written word. The craft intrigues me. Novel ideas and bookshelves excite me. I value making written accounts of my internal and external worlds.

Sometimes writing and I have altercations, but we always reunite to continue the journey. I miss writing when I'm away from it because I give to my words and my words give back. We grow with each other.

All these things make me a writer rather than whether I've written a best seller, or write full time, or have made any money out of my writing projects yet.

Whenever I state I'm a writer the reality strengthens, my heart beats faster, and I feel true to myself.

Affirmation

I am a writer. Writing is more than a profession, an art, or a past time. It's my nature. So I write here and now.

I write for the dreams I envision. I write from my head, heart, and soul. I write because it helps me evolve. I write to make my higher self happy. I write to share my identity and my understanding. I write because it's what I want to do with my life.

I'm proud to be a writer at every stage of my development. Writing takes guts. Writing takes grunt. I hereby declare that I am a writer.

~ Insight 3 ~

Words Count

The most important first step to my writing success is meeting my daily word count. Writing a set word quota every day ensures that a first draft builds up fast and keeps me in tune with it.

Writing daily keeps me on track with plots and consistent with characters, writing style, and mood. It saves me time re-reading my material to work out where I left off.

Reaching my daily word count rewards me with momentum and motivation to finish the first draft. It creates a habit that helps to remove any reluctance to write.

I write a set number of words per day despite where I am or how tired, blocked, or distracted I may feel. Completing my word quota is a sacred ritual that I perform religiously because it keeps me on the road to my writing dreams.

My daily word count is a number that suits where I'm at right now with writing and my life. If my goal is two hundred words a day and I continue to reach this target, I'll have a 73,000 word draft novel in a year's time. I can build up the amount as I get more time to write and/or as I build up. Writing is like exercise. The more I write, the more I'll want to.

Writing begets more writing, which creates more finished manuscripts, produces more submissions and/or online publications, brings about more opportunities for acceptances and/or sales, and leads to more writing success. Honouring my daily word count helps me experience the professional writer's life.

Writing is one of my life's purposes so meeting my daily word count is a top priority. I commit to my daily goal to satisfy a need that belongs to my higher self and to enjoy watching my projects grow.

Affirmation

I meet my daily word count because this step is critical to my writing success. When I reach a set minimum word requirement every day I demonstrate commitment to my dreams. It also helps me maintain the motivation and enthusiasm I need to finish the first draft and get the project to the next stage of development. I write daily to strengthen the professional writer's habit in me and to help remove any reluctance to write.

Whenever I reach my daily word quota I keep a personal promise and satisfy a creative need that belongs to my higher self. This makes my soul happy.

~ Insight 4 ~

Come What May

At times I may feel frustrated with my progress and achievements, but I've grown to realise that I'm unable to quit writing because it's a large, deep part of me. Sometimes it feels like writing is all I have. Therefore, I must accept writing into my life and embrace it. Making the decision to keep writing, whatever the results, ends any need for further internal debate and this gives me a sense of peace.

Like most writers with commercial aspirations I want to multi-publish, receive recognition, and enjoy financial reward for my work. However, I write for more than this. I write for the love, creativity, intrigue, and challenge of it. If I wrote only for the former reasons, commercial success would be unattainable because I'd be lacking the heart to write. Therefore, I take the journey and any setbacks in my stride rather than pine longingly for the dream destination.

My relationship with writing is unconditional and this liberates me from the heavy shackles I used to put on myself and on my writing to produce the results I crave. My resolute bond with the craft helps to free my creative spirit and gives me the mind-set to write without fretting about the outcome.

Affirmation

I write for more than public acclaim and profits. I write to make my higher self happy since writing is part of me. I write for the experience as well as for the destination. Therefore, I travel along the writing journey with a calm, resolute outlook despite disappointments.

My relationship with writing is unconditional and so I take joy in my decision to keep writing come what may. I feel strong and at peace because I've resolved the matter.

~ Insight 5 ~

Other Ways to Count

There are times when meeting my daily word count is irrelevant to the stage I'm at with a writing project. I may have met my daily word count for weeks or months and finished the first draft which I now need to edit.

Most writers agree that editing is eighty percent of the work required to produce a publication-worthy manuscript. Writing the first draft then is a small part of the big picture. There are the tasks of rearranging, adjusting, amending, and pruning every draft up to and including the final draft to render it as perfect as possible for seamless reading.

Then there's the process of letting the final draft sit for a while and re-reading it with fresh eyes to test whether I get bogged by any part of the story or snagged on any sentences and ambiguities.

After the final draft is complete, I need to prepare for online publishing and/or traditional submission. There's also the promotion and marketing to nut out.

Therefore, my daily writing goal may change from meeting my word count to editing a fixed number of pages per day. Or my daily target could be to complete individual set tasks like finding the best shout line for my novel cover or fixing my online publication layout so it complies with recommendations and guidelines. To ensure steady progress I could stick to a number of hours per day to work on a project.

If I set a minimum daily time requirement I allow myself the flexibility and goal measurement I need to tackle any stage or area of the project I wish. At least an hour or two with a couple of short breaks is preferable, but this could be divided into smaller stints of say fifteen minutes throughout the day if necessary.

A minimum requirement of an hour per day helps me accomplish marked project development and, like the daily word count goal, enables me to stay in tune with the project while maintaining momentum and enthusiasm.

Affirmation

I have many ways in which to determine and measure my daily writing goal. I adjust the goal type to suit each stage of project development, but two things remain the same: I attend to my writing dreams on a daily basis and take great delight in watching the project grow into a finished creation, ready for the marketplace.

~ Insight 6 ~

Explore

Genres classify different types of literature that share common criteria. The simplest and broadest division is the fiction or fabricated story and non-fiction or fact genres.

Greek philosophers Aristotle and Plato divided the fiction genre into drama, poetry, and prose. Today the prose genre divides into many narrower genres or sub-categories such as romance, science fiction, horror, erotica, fantasy, historical fiction, adventure, comedy, crime, faction, mystery, action, paranoid, paranormal, philosophical, saga, urban and more. Most of these have further sub-categories and many contain a blend of genres such as adventure fantasy. Examples of non-fiction genres are biography, autobiography, self-help, cooking, travel, and education. A readership age or format, such as a children's book or graphic novel, does not define a genre.

I explore different genres to find the ones that stir me with passion. This entails identifying genre criteria, requirements, and readership, the information of which I can find online. It also involves experimenting by writing in various categories to find which types feel most natural to me. A good idea is to read a cross-section of works in the genres that interest me and heed what published authors say about writing in their chosen fields.

Broadening my understanding of genres deepens my writing knowledge and experience. It fosters my appreciation and understanding of all writers. I refrain from judging genres that I have yet to examine and accept that trial and error comes with experimentation.

Affirmation

I research and experiment with different genres to find the ones that fire me up the most and that I feel best writing. This is part of discovering the authentic writer in me so that my writing may shine to its full potential.

Testing out genres helps me determine the type of writing journey I want to go on and gives my future endeavours clear direction before I proceed.

I have more than one preferred genre in order to broaden my portfolio of work and increase the opportunities available to me. A little diversity also helps keep my writing journey fun and interesting along the way.

~ Insight 7 ~

The Visible Workout

I balance the sedentary act of writing with routine physical exercise to enable me to write regularly. Physical activity gives my mind a break from heavy or repetitive thoughts, strengthens the communication pathways between my brain and body, and sends bursts of oxygen to my parameters.

Going for a walk helps me to slip into a semi-subconscious state which can open my mind's barriers and let in solutions to all sorts of challenges. My outlook tends to clear and I receive fresh ideas with the intake of fresh air and surroundings. I also get a dose of Vitamin D from sunshine which strengthens my bones and helps me hold a seated position with good posture for longer periods. Writers who write daily and at length indoors can be prone to Vitamin D deficiency.

Sitting for long periods can cause circulation problems, muscle strain, and fatigue. Therefore, I provide myself with an ergonomic writing environment and ample lighting. I wear correct glasses if necessary. I keep my feet warm and take short breaks from writing at least every fifty minutes so I can complete any length writing project I want with as little discomfort as possible.

During the short writing breaks I stretch my body, especially my neck, shoulders, lower back, and legs. I expand my lungs because my breathing may shorten and become shallower while I write. Oxygen helps to keep me alert.

I limit my caffeine and sugar intake to increase calmness and reduce irritability. I drink lots of water and opt for healthy snacks during writing periods.

I get plenty of sleep so my brain can be in better condition to fire on all synapses. My attitude to writing tends to be more positive if I'm well-rested and free from toxins; my thoughts become more effective at making new connections and good decisions. My alertness can reach an optimum level which assists me in locating the areas of my work that need improvement.

It's wise to put my best foot forwards in order to increase the overall quality of my writing experience and extend my writing capacity.

Affirmation

I exercise regularly and get enough sleep to help me live a happy writer's life. Physical activity increases my ability to focus and decreases discomfort so I take frequent short breaks during writing periods. I attend to my health and watch my diet for general wellbeing and this helps to increase my writing output and quality. I avoid overindulgence. I listen to my body and respond to its needs so that it can serve me well in life and support my long term writing.

~ Insight 8 ~

The Invisible Workout

The 'non-writers' around me can find it hard to comprehend my chronic need to sit motionless in isolation and fixate on a piece of paper or a screen. Their unconscious facial expressions often reveal that writing to them is an act of self-imposed solitary confinement and torture. Their tilted heads indicate that it's difficult for them to fathom how a great day to me is when I'm free to write without any social commitments or sporting events in the way.

It may be hard for extroverts to agree that chatting for hours is a waste of precious writing time or that socialising is put to better use by observing human behaviour, settings, and dialogues for writing purposes. That's fine.

The 'non-writers' have yet to feel the rush of the writer's flow, the subconsciousness stream. They are unaware that sometimes when I write I catch alight: my mind is ablaze, the synapses spark, the emotions burn, and the creativity crackles.

Sometimes when I write I fill up with psychedelic swirls and my imagination transforms into a pulsing, productive organ. I can become enthralled for hours by the self-generating entertainment. The unseen connection between my mind, body, and soul is pulling ethereal thoughts into the earth plane out through my fingertips.

So much invisible stuff happens when I write because my soul is doing most of the work. It's okay if 'non-writers' are unable to feel what I feel and relate to my need to write. Sometimes I'm unable to experience joy from activities that others do.

Affirmation

I accept that writers and 'non-writers' have different compositions, outlooks, and needs. I let this disparity go because the world requires all types of people for it to function. Lots of invisible processes and sensations occur when I write so it's natural that 'non-writers' may find it difficult to relate. I smile and let it be.

~ Insight 9 ~

Alternative Routes to Success

There are other roads to success besides writing a bestselling novel or the timeless picture book. Therefore, I refuse to restrict myself to these two avenues. There are many kinds of accomplished writers and lots of them are unknown to the public. So I'm open to the wide variety of writing opportunities that can help me establish my writing career.

Fiction book publishing is only one mode of transportation I can use to arrive at writing success in the public domain. To broaden my options I visit websites and explore the many ways in which I could write professionally and earn an income.

I could look into writing: copy, greeting cards, newspaper columns, brochures, press releases, children's activity and puzzle books, magazine articles, newsletters, comics, graphic novels, scripts, educational books, how-to e-books about a niche area I know and love, short stories for anthologies or magazines, résumés, speeches, blogs, websites, TV shows and more.

Affirmation

I consider the vast writing opportunities that lie beyond authoring the great novel or picture book. I have many alternative routes to success. I can become a profitable writer without having to be famous.

I'm open to earning income from different types of writing and refuse to limit my sources. I have the conviction to be a writer and stay on the journey, whichever routes I take.

~ Insight 10 ~

Please My Higher Self

My higher self loves to help people. My higher self loves to communicate through the written word. Both acts can be therapeutic for the soul and bring revelations. Both acts can serve others and express my higher self. However, my soul can feel unbalanced if only one act tends to dominate my time and energy. Therefore, it's okay to balance helping people with time spent writing in order to keep my higher self happy and my spirits lifted.

I can refuse someone's request for assistance if it means that I'm unable to do the writing I had my heart set on for the day. It's okay to offer an alternative time that better suits me. It's alright to agree to help provided I get some writing done first.

If I keep attending to others' needs by pushing writing aside I may end up resenting the help I give and the recipient will feel this negativity. Or people may take me for granted if I'm constantly available to help them achieve their goals over mine.

I help keep my energy high and positive when I attend to all my higher self's desires using a balanced approach. This energy enables me to write in greater quantity and higher quality. It allows me to help others more effectively in a better frame of mind.

When I honour my soul's needs I'm a better person to be around and the positive energy helps facilitate faster, more productive outcomes. I please my higher self by being balanced because it's for the higher good of all concerned.

Affirmation

I balance my need to help people with my need to write. This is a safeguard I use to keep my higher self content. I attend to all my soul's desires in equal measure to enjoy an ongoing sense of deep fulfilment and happiness. This way I'm able to give to others wholeheartedly and keep the writing promises I make to myself. Writing is one of my spirit's real needs and so I must honour it regularly with action.

~ Insight 11 ~

Nurture Talent and Hone Skills

Just as a natural singer needs to sing, a painter to paint, a sculptor to sculpt and an actor to act, I'm a writer who must write. And, like all of these artisans, I need to practise my craft regularly to go from good to outstanding.

I give myself writing tasks that I complete. I rehearse putting ideas into words to refine my natural ability and attune my unique writing voice. I learn how to better cultivate my skills through acquiring information and then I apply the knowledge to my work in a methodical manner. I learn how to prune my writing in the right places so it can blossom to its full potential. I develop a bird's eye for spotting bugs, twigs, and dead leaves in my work.

I accept the fact that all forms of natural talent require ongoing devotion in order to produce creations of excellence. Regular practice enables the owners of the instruments to become masterful and reap the rewards of outstanding performance. As a writer, I accept that I'm party to this and so I willingly practise, practise, practise.

Affirmation

I nurture my talent and hone my skills to become a writing maestro. I practise writing regularly, applying the tools from the ever increasing knowledge I acquire. Every day in every way my work improves and writing well becomes easier.

With devotion and passion I do what it takes to progress from being a great writer to an outstanding wordsmith.

~ Insight 12 ~

Write For the Right Reasons

It's imperative to know why I write and why certain writing genres appeal to me. This base understanding and clarification help increase the value I put on my writing.

Knowing why I write helps to motivate me to write regularly and increases my commitment to projects. Writing becomes a need, rather than a want.

Being specific about whom I want to write for and why refines the target and reinforces my focus. This guides me to stay on the straight path and write with clear aim.

I have greater prospects of success when I write upon the correct knowledge of why I write. There are many reasons I could have for writing such as:

- To serve others,
- To connect with others,
- For financial reward,
- For public validation,
- For dream fulfilment,
- For the privilege of entering a reader's world and impacting on it,
- For the therapeutic effects on my head, heart, and soul,
- For the joy of creating something out of nothing,

- To improve and excel at the craft, for the art of it,
- Because I can,
- Because I care,
- To be heard and for others to be heard through me,
- Because I feel compelled since writing is my nature and an inseparable component of my life,
- Because it pleases my higher self,
- Because it keeps me pre-occupied and out of trouble,
- To explore the human condition, reveal aspects of it, and offer understanding,
- Because it surprises, entertains, and intrigues me,
- Because every project is a thrilling, unchartered adventure,
- Because I have a strong affinity with certain genres and their readerships.

Affirmation

I have a list of reasons why I write and I'm clear about what they are. The reasons fuel me to write. The grounds upon which I write are strong and purposeful, therefore writing is worthy of my time and effort. My motives for writing help give me the staying power to succeed. My most powerful reason is that writing pleases my spirit and is an inseparable part of me.

That alone is reason enough to write with aspirations and have faith that I'll achieve them.

~ Insight 13 ~

The Yellow Brick Roads

We can liken the traditional publisher to 'The Wizard of Oz'. It once controlled writers' destinies. Writers once believed The Wizard was the only power that could help them achieve their ultimate dreams, although the yellow brick road was long, winding, and potholed leading to a virtually non-existent publication offer.

Traditional publishers have rejected ninety-nine percent of writers' proposals for years and will probably continue to do so. Writers have had to wait months to receive standard rejection responses with many publishers further restricting writers by refusing multiple and/or simultaneous submissions.

Online self-publishing has provided an alternative yellow brick road which fast tracks writers to publication, unrestricted potential, and self-reliance. It's evident that The Wizard of Oz has become a diminished power unable to hide its vulnerability behind curtains anymore.

Writers can now publish alongside The Wizard, learn to market effectively, have control over their own work, and receive instant gratification from royalties instead of waiting, in some cases, for years to get payment from traditional publishers.

Many publishing houses' websites indicate that they have changed their tune towards writers now that writers possess the power to self-publish for little or no cost with much higher royalty percentages. Traditional publishers seem to be making their submission guidelines more writer friendly and with a warmer disposition are inviting writers to submit.

Traditional publishers in general appear to be allowing shorter, easier submissions, but want to know more about the author to ascertain whether he or she has a pre-established position online and offline in the marketplace to advance book sales. Today, the popularity that an online book has already gained may convince a traditional publisher to take the book on.

It seems that the surest way to a traditional publisher's heart is to self-publish, create an online presence and following, establish significant sales and/or interest in the book, and then propose the book to the publisher with the supporting results. Or otherwise win a publisher's writing competition.

Some traditional publishers, like Penguin, now open their doors for specific types of books at particular times of the year, at last providing a guide to writers as to what the publishers want and when. Other publishers, like Allen and Unwin via its Friday Pitch, open their doors to ideas on a weekly or monthly basis in a bid to process and extract proposals that may be worthwhile investigating as fast as possible.

The online publishing methods give glorious freedom to today's writer, but this facilitates a crowded market in which to compete. In turn this tends to lower the price of books and allows inferior writing into the marketplace. So besides self-promotion the quality of my end product must be high enough to give it the integrity that a traditionally published book would have in order to stand above mediocre publications.

It's vital that I'm a tough self-editor or have a qualified editor go through my product before I publish it online. If I'm unable to afford someone to scrutinise my book, I could offer an English major student or writer friend an editor acknowledgement on the front cover and/or payment dependent on the sales rather than upfront.

Affirmation

I'm free to become a self-published author for little or no cost. I'm no longer bound by the constraints of the traditional and vanity publishing industries.

However, in following this alternative yellow brick road I understand that now I'm also the publisher's editor-in-chief and must oversee the quality of my work using the best approach I can and in the strictest sense to produce a high end product that will fulfil readers' expectations. I also accept that the onus is entirely on me to promote and sell my work.

~ Insight 14 ~

Build Up Knowledge

I continue to build upon my concept of writing. It takes time to acquire and internalise information about its many aspects, but I avoid letting this process obstruct me from meeting my daily writing goal and deadlines.

As a side line activity to writing, I read authors' works in the genres that excite me to write. I observe their techniques, voices, similarities, and differences. I contemplate which style of writing I think is better and why.

I make time to read and re-read library and online books, articles, self-help e-books, writers' blogs, publishers' websites, and industry newsletters to learn about how to write well and what constitutes professional, profitable writing.

I keep building upon my writing knowledge to remain up to date with changes, developments, and new information. Sometimes the same information presented in a different way will hit home harder and cause the penny to drop so it's productive to read about the same topics by different authors.

I use a thesaurus and dictionary often to check the meanings and synonyms of words to strengthen my understanding of how and when to use them in my work.

When other writers recommend particular writing programs I investigate to ascertain whether such programs could assist me.

As I continue to build upon my writing knowledge, my conscious and subconscious take in the elements and piece them together into an overall picture. In time I'll become better attuned to the areas of my work that I could improve based on the solid foundation of my ever expanding knowledge.

Affirmation

There seems to be so much to get right with writing, but that's okay. All the information will fall into place if I keep reading and writing.

The more knowledge I gain about writing the deeper and broader my understanding of it will become, helping me to create higher end quality products.

My overall concept of writing is forever growing, stabilising, and refining. I can see and feel the impact that the information has on my work and this excites me.

~ Insight 15 ~

Belief Power

I write a set of empowering beliefs that merges the prosperity and joy I experience each day with what I want to achieve. This helps me feel the richness I derive from my own present actions rather than relying on abundance from the future or circumstances that may be out of my control.

My empowering beliefs allow me to redefine the meaning of writing if writing has become a chore. The drafts, the research, the submission process, the rejections, the isolation and so on can feel like a hard slog if I've digressed to writing purely for financial reward or public acclaim. I may need to change the way I see writing to enjoy the journey again. I may need to return to feeling the joys of writing and accepting the challenges from a more positive perspective.

Thoughts are powerful. Repetition of thoughts helps to instil my belief in them so I repeat my empowering beliefs often to brand them into my subconscious and fortify my belief system.

Example of my empowering beliefs:

I believe in myself and my dreams. I believe in my loved ones and their dreams. We are wealthy because we share our love, support, strengths, and ideas every day.

There is a force field of protection around me and my family at all times. It comes from the universe and protects us from all harm.

I'm a prosperous, published children's writer and entrepreneur. Every year I produce a popular, profitable children's book. I write every day to give myself and readers joy and satisfaction. Writing completes me. It lights me up.

My writing creates wealth for me and others. My words inspire, help, heal, understand, make action happen, move people, manifest dreams, achieve goals, excite and enchant, unite people, entertain and engage people, show people, teach people, love people, and make money.

Exciting ideas for children's stories come to me freely and frequently from the universe. Words flow from me onto the page. Solutions to plot problems appear whenever I need them.

My family, my time, my words, my goals, my health, my thoughts, my talents, my work, my humour, my will, and my possessions all form my wealth. I'm already rich.

Every day in every way I become better and better, happier, healthier, wiser, wealthier, and more balanced. I move towards tomorrow calmly and with confidence.

Affirmation

I create a set of empowering beliefs that focuses on what I want to attract and achieve. My empowering beliefs remind me that I'm already wealthy in so many ways. They help me feel the joy in what I do and have already. I use them to assure myself and condition my outlook.

I remove any difficult terms I place on writing to help reinstate the pleasure I get from it. This makes it easier for me to write and deal with challenges.

I achieve the dreams that I believe I can. Therefore, I repeat my empowering beliefs several times daily to help instil a strong belief system that will carry me to my dreams.

~ Insight 16 ~

The Alpha and the Omega

A negative attitude can act like boom gates and stop my writing in its tracks. This happens when I focus on the struggles instead of fantasising about the dream. To make a mental road block disappear I need to make a conscious effort to turn away from the boom gates and bells and look out in a different direction that has an unobstructed view.

I can focus on the satisfaction I'll feel when I finish the chapter. I can seize the opportunity right now to complete the next page. I can rub my hands together and wonder what might pour out of me next. I can change my line of thinking from *what's the point?* or *what if I can't?* simply to *what if?* and feel showered by possibilities. Or I can switch to an easier writing project to get me going again.

A shift in attitude is a shift in energy: a shift from slumping in front of a hurdle to powering across the finish line, a shift from staring into a microscope to gazing through binoculars, a shift in seeing a project as perhaps a waste of time to one that is imperative to complete, a shift from what I have failed to achieve so far to what I have yet to achieve, and a shift from despondency to delight.

Attitude is a double-edged sword that I must continually wield with care; it can save or kill the writer in me.

Affirmation

Before I sit down to write I assess where my attitude is on the spectrum of positivity and deliberately adjust it to facilitate writing. I reverse a negative attitude by reinforcing what I have set out to do and why. I focus on accomplishing the next small goal. My solar plexus can then stir with excitement instead of panging with apprehension. The boom gates and warning bells disappear and I can proceed full steam ahead on my writing journey.

My attitude is the alpha and the omega, the beginning and the end, eternally affecting everything I do.

~ Insight 17 ~

Score Goals

I set myself specific long and short term writing goals. These goals draw a daily response from me, big or small. I visualise achieving my dreams and even though some of them are lofty I'm unconcerned because I believe that anything's possible. Life has its twists and turns. If I only achieve seventy-five percent of my dreams I'd be ecstatic.

I'm unfazed if I miss a goal because striving for it has kept me writing and moving forwards on the journey. Goals that super stretch me fling me far ahead even if I fall short. It's okay for some goals to take longer to achieve than expected if I feel I awarded them the attention and time they deserved.

I persevere towards my writing dreams by keeping the bigger picture in mind. I concentrate on completing the smaller goals that lead to its attainment. I take pragmatic steps daily in the direction of my dreams and pat myself on the back whenever I finish a task.

Success is more than reaching the final destination. Rather, success is a constant component of the journey meaning that I acknowledge the achievements along the way. Every sized goal I attain is a reason to celebrate success.

My most important writing goal is to write or edit every day and I honour this goal to the best of my ability. This is part of my routine whether it means I have to get up an hour earlier, go to bed an hour later, write on a train or during my lunch break.

Affirmation

The big picture fires me up. The smaller goals are the stepping stones to my dreams so I value them and acknowledge their attainment.

I set down small goals with timeframes and deadlines and commit myself to them. I use the small goals to help me get to the next stage and ultimately fulfil a long term plan of action. I celebrate every writing goal I achieve, great or small, because the attainment of each one is a measure of my success.

~ Insight 18 ~

Respond Rather Than React

The online source www.health.com states that writing is one of the top ten professions most likely to lead to depression so I guard against letting the challenges of writing get me down and hold me there. I'm careful to choose my responses to situations rather than let my reactions rule. I do my best to thwart any negative urges and instead respond in a productive manner that's good for my mental and emotional health.

I become equipped to handle issues such as self-doubt, rejection, obscurity, isolation, imminent deadlines, obsessive desire, the critics, executive changes, the public eye, creative block, unfamiliar technology, the uncertainty of financial reward and so on by understanding that these elements may rain upon all writers at various times. They are part of the writer's journey and that of the artist's journey in general so I acknowledge this and refuse to let such challenges blow me over. Otherwise, I may as well leave the game.

I'm informed about the obstacles that could lie ahead. The writer's journey can be a tricky road to follow so I cloak myself with mental and emotional protection in preparation. One way I do this is by monitoring my behaviour and conditioning my responses to adversity. I work on my resilience and respond rather than react.

Affirmation

I'm in charge of my emotions. I'm bigger than they are because I decide the extent of power they have over my actions and thoughts. I choose how I respond to obstacles, setbacks, losses, and issues. I acknowledge my emotions, but keep my eyes on the dreams. I handle negative emotions by learning to use them in a positive way. For example, I convert anger energy into constructive action.

I remain open to the opportunities that may appear along my writing journey instead of letting my emotions close me off to them. I respond rather than react as a means of self-preservation.

~ Insight 19 ~

Build Up a Calendar

I build up a calendar consisting of competition deadlines, publisher submission dates, online self-publishing award dates, writers' festival weeks, and closing dates for writers' grants so that I can foresee the events and participate if I wish. I find these opportunities by searching online including government and library websites, in local papers, and by subscribing to various industry newsletters.

My writing calendar can inspire me to take on a range of writing tasks and help me keep writing all year round. Selecting events to engage in makes me feel purposeful, goal orientated, and in the game. A new deadline may prompt me to take on a new genre or project.

The calendar also encourages me to get mileage out of my work; if I'm unsuccessful with a submission I can check when and where else to submit the same piece instead of stowing it away in a drawer or closed computer file.

Every finished writing product takes time and effort to create and deserves to see the light of day for a while. Therefore, I allow my writing pieces to run the gauntlet of open avenues available to them, which in turn helps me assess where my writing may be at and speculate as to where it could improve.

Circulating my work keeps me pumped with adrenalin. I might succeed on the next submission. I might gain acknowledgement for that piece. I might win a prize and enjoy a financial return for my efforts. A calendar of writing event dates is like a Christmas Advent Calendar since every date has the ability to bring a sweet reward.

Affirmation

I build up a calendar of writing dates to keep my eye on the sweet possibilities ahead of me and to keep my current pieces circulating. I subscribe to and read industry newsletters. I take some time to find writing opportunities online and around my community. I match my existing writing pieces to what I find.

I love throwing myself at a writing challenge and rising to meet its deadline. I enjoy participating and submitting my work. Therefore, I use my writing calendar as a tool to help me locate the opportunities in time to prepare for them properly.

~ Insight 20 ~

Success Appeal

I need to write about character ordeals that would have a strong impact on most readers in order to have the best chance of widespread public success. I need a story that will connect with the majority, rather than the minority, of people.

Writing for a large common readership may seem like I have to write about a general topic from a baseline, common perspective to create universal appeal, but rather I need to do the opposite. Instead, I attract a large readership's attention by using a fresh perspective, a new angle, and heightened predicaments so that readers can experience commonly shared emotions in a different light. I can do this using any theme or topic.

Also, to appeal to the masses, my writing needs to be succinct and accurate enough to convey the fresh perspective globally. My communication needs to be so straight forward and unambiguous that every reader is likely to get the same story. The writing has to be good enough to affect many people in exactly the same way at exactly the same points in the story.

The better I'm able to write clearly from a new angle on a theme to which most people can relate and about ordeals that have impact, the greater the chance of capturing a large readership's interest.

Affirmation

I write in an unambiguous manner that encourages every reader to relate and respond to my story in a similar way. I make my writing so clear that it elicits the same emotions from readers at the same points in the story. I can write about topics and predicaments that may be unfamiliar to many readers as long as my writing emotionally and uniformly connects them with the characters, characters' experiences, and the theme.

~ Insight 21 ~

Reject Rejection

The pledge to keep writing helps me overcome the disappointment of a rejection letter or a critical online review. The hot resolve to continue writing no matter what melts rejection's cold, steel grip. The pain quickly subsides because I've scrapped the internal debate. The indecision is over.

I'm level headed enough to consider what may have led to the rejection from an objective viewpoint. I'm wise enough to know that there are many reasons for a publisher to reject a proposal. Some of these reasons are out of my control such as an editor's moods, publishing cutbacks, or a recent publication with a similar perspective as mine.

Everyone is entitled to his or her view. I handle any unfavourable online ratings and readers' comments by reading them at arm's length, rather than as a personal attack. This part of my writing journey could make me and my writing stronger if I consider the criticisms fairly. It's unrealistic to regard myself as perfect, so I consider any frustration I might feel from objective comments to be normal rather than devastating.

It can be difficult to read my work from a stranger's viewpoint when I've been immersed in the project. It's impossible to please every reader. I accept that I can always improve a piece and I thank any critical readers for taking the time to read my work and comment on it.

All writers experience rejection along the journey. The ones who deal with it move onwards and upwards.

Affirmation

Rejection hurts, but I shake it out of my system and move on. It has no hold over me. My vow to keep writing removes the temptation to feel sorry for myself and quit. I've already decided to stay true to my dreams and this overpowers any feelings of rejection I may experience.

Whether a publisher rejects my work or the populace criticises it I'm mature enough to accept that no-one owes me anything and that my ideas and writing pieces are simply proposals put forth into the world.

~ Insight 22 ~

Embrace Technology and Change

I embrace the technology available to me and the changes taking place in the publishing industry. Today I have greater power to earn greater profits via online self-publishing and I'm open to this avenue as an alternative to traditional and vanity publishing.

I invest time into learning how to use technology and the internet to my writing advantage. I look into writing programs that assist today's writer and explore social media and networking opportunities.

I research how to publish online Print On Demand books (POD), Kindle books, and e-books. I incorporate a website/blog that is generous to my visitors and makes me accessible worldwide. I consider the crowd-funding opportunities available from websites such as pozible.com and kickstarter.com. I learn about social media and how to use it to promote myself and my work.

Technology is meant to aid me rather than overwhelm me so I put any reservations aside and take the time to explore new technological advancements that can assist me as a writer, using a positive, patient attitude.

Affirmation

Technology is here to help me so I jump in and look around. However, I learn how to use it step by step in a calm and methodical manner. I invest the time I need to demystify technology so I can make well-informed decisions and take the best action for my writing projects.

I'm blessed to be a writer in today's world because the technology and industry that exist make it so much easier for me to write, publish, promote, and sell my work globally. I have millions of potential readers within my reach.

~ Insight 23 ~

The Best Policy

I write true to myself, meaning that my output is honest. I write without malice, but also without worrying whether the content will upset someone. It's alright for others to disagree with me. We all have our own realities and truths. We all have our opinions and individual experiences. This is what it is to be human.

Writing from the heart may also connect me to collective consciousness. By tuning into myself I might intuit the waves of commonly shared feelings, beliefs, and ideas that are emanating from society, which my writing could help bring to light and unify.

When I write truthfully it encourages readers to consider my interpretations of life with a degree of trust even if they have a different opinion at the outset or conclude that what I've written opposes their views.

Affirmation

I write with honesty about the world and the human condition. This allows me to remain true to my perceptions and instil trust in the reader. If I write with truth and without ego, my words can become powerful yet gentle enough for readers to open up and contemplate them. Likewise, I expand my own understanding of humankind and the world through the work of other honest writers.

~ Insight 24 ~

Juggle and Balance

Writing is a craft that requires a lot of time. Sometimes I may feel guilty about how much time I spend writing if it takes me away from family and friends for extended periods. When I work longer and harder to meet a writing deadline I may fret about neglecting responsibilities and setting other priorities aside. For example, my home may start to reflect the lack of my attention. Balance is the key to life and during intense writing periods it may feel like I've dropped the ball.

However, I can use a longer time frame to measure whether I'm living a balanced life and juggling all responsibilities well. I can consider concentrated writing periods in a broader context. I can compare the ratio of writing to meeting other responsibilities over a block of weeks or months rather than over several days. After all, there tends to be times when other obligations demand my attention and push my writing towards the back of the line.

The overall picture shows me that I put much time and energy into helping others achieve their goals, attending to life's demands, and meeting non-writing commitments. Therefore, it's unnecessary for me to feel guilty about the periods during which I put extra hours and effort into writing to help me achieve my goals.

Affirmation

In the grand scheme of things I balance my attention across all commitments. In the long run I meet every responsibility, including the duty to myself to work towards my writing dreams.

It's okay to fixate on writing to meet a deadline and achieve a goal. It's alright if there are times when writing demands my focus for longer periods than usual. Sometimes this sort of juggling is what it takes to help me fulfil my writing aspirations. I know that I'll restore everyday balance again soon.

~ Insight 25 ~

Invite Lord Maitreya

Lord Maitreya is known to be an Ascended Master who holds the office of World Teacher in the metaphysical realm. He oversees humankind's evolution and offers truths about existence. I invite him by my side and ask that his vibrations help me reveal teachings and truths in my writing.

I ask Lord Maitreya to energise me to write if I feel depleted. I request that he help me raise my level of consciousness so I can get in touch with my higher self to write more clearly, easily, and with purpose.

Words flow freely from my fingers when I let go of self-consciousness and write from a subconscious place. This is the heavenly way to write. I ask Lord Maitreya to help me achieve the state in which I may write in this manner.

I call upon a working partnership between my rational and creative thinking that allows my creativity to step forwards and speak without self-judgement or censorship from my rational faculty.

I ask Lord Maitreya to bless the deep thinkers across the world and inspire them to come up with new creative ideas to share with and benefit others.

Affirmation

I summon my subconscious to come to the fore and facilitate the divine writing flow because this is the happiest and purest way in which to write. I ask my rationality to step aside and put self-consciousness on hold.

I call upon Lord Maitreya's loving vibrations to soothe and replenish me. I'm open to receiving higher knowledge and truths so I may relay them through writing. I ask the Ascended Master to help me, my writing, and my world evolve. I thank Lord Maitreya for his guidance and influence.

~ Insight 26 ~

From Topic to Toe

Publishing house editors tend to agree that ninety-nine percent of the unsolicited manuscripts they receive is unpublishable due to basic common flaws. These faults include typographical errors, incorrect grammar, wrong punctuation, misuse of homonyms, use of tired clichés, improper layout, erratic pacing, changing points of view, two dimensional characters, passive and poor writing, nonsensical endings, hackneyed plots and more.

In the self-publishing world, writing flaws in an online chapter sample will deter readers from buying my book.

If I take care to eliminate the most common and basic faults from my work the reader or editor will look beyond the writing to the content, perspective, and voice, as they should, in order to make the decision to buy or accept my book for publication. An editor or online buyer needs to feel confident when they read a sample and must form the expectation that my writing will deliver. Therefore, I get the nuts and bolts of my writing correct and render my product professional enough for publication.

Editors also reject manuscripts because the topic or theme is unsuitable for their publishing list or the story is too similar to what they have recently published. So I do my best to write about a topic, theme, and/or storyline that's refreshing, alluring, and appropriate for the intended market. I could write about a current published topic or theme, but the perspective must be from a new angle.

I study publishing lists, genre criteria, and what's available out there already to help me speculate whether my book idea will hit the target audience. I find out what makes a manuscript professional and attune my writing to this. My publishable work must accommodate an identifiable, viable audience for the chance of market success and income.

Affirmation

I take great care with the presentation and content of my work so that the world will take a chance on me and read it. I lift myself into the top one percent of writers by eliminating the most common fundamental weaknesses from my writing. I target the contents of my project to the intended market with deliberation and accuracy to give myself the opportunity to sell to happy customers.

~ Insight 27 ~

Keep a Lookout

I remind myself that my loved ones live with the writer in me although they did not sign up for the writer's journey. Therefore, during the ups and downs of my writing life, I refrain from throwing my writer's weight around.

I acknowledge that to protect the emotional wellbeing of the closest people to me I need to select how I respond to writing setbacks and victories. Any writing obstacle I encounter can negatively affect my emotions and behaviour if I let it. Therefore, I claim any adverse experiences as my own and remember that they lie along the path that I've chosen. I refuse to let any triumphs go to my head.

I understand that friends and family may find it tough to watch me invest time and energy without much return. I appreciate how the people in my life accommodate the reclusive me and that sometimes as a writer I may appear self-important.

However, by being a writer who never gives up or feels sorry for myself I demonstrate to the people around me the strength of the dream, the walking of the walk, and the artist's resolve to remain true to oneself. I keep a vigilant look out for family and friends and take great care to give them a positive experience of the aspiring writer's life.

Affirmation

I'm mature in handling writing disappointments. I'm mindful of my behaviour during setbacks and struggles. I do my best to choose my responses to minimise any negative impact on loved ones. I'm level-headed when I experience success. I make living with an aspiring writer a pleasurable experience by demonstrating persistence, resilience, positivity, and passion.

~ Insight 28 ~

Competition

Sometimes I might feel that the competition is too great for my writing to shine or that the winning streak has left me. The reality is that I put a lot of hard work into writing as do a multitude of talented writers. However, I refuse to quit as I'm unable to see around career corners. Also, I'm one of a kind.

I keep participating because maybe I just missed making the shortlist last time. I keep online publishing because it gives me a thrill and I enjoy writing. I keep submitting because I have to be in it to win it. I have a go because my unique life experiences and perceptions set me apart from other writers.

I can only win if I submit my best and most suited pieces, polished to a professional standard. I must ensure I follow submission guidelines to the letter. I make my competition entry, industry submission, or online self-publication publishable in every sense which helps to lift me into the top one percent of contenders. Then it's up to my unique voice and my take on life to pull me through to victory.

Whenever I revisit my work months later I always find areas to improve. I'm matter of fact about this, rather than feel dejected. When I see my work at arm's length its weaknesses jump out at me and I realise why it may not have been the competition winner, the accepted submission, or the high selling self-publication. If I'm strong enough to own this I can further develop the piece as long as I still believe it has promise and my enthusiasm is strong.

My writing's evolution runs in tandem with my writing journey and evolves with me. As a more experienced writer I can rework an old piece and resubmit it. However, I avoid revisiting a manuscript that's very old because I would've changed and grown so much since writing it that revision would be a nightmare and a waste of time.

Affirmation

There's competition out there, but that's okay. Every submission, entry, and self-publication I undertake strengthens my skills and resilience. I persist and stay in the game because the writer who wins is the writer who never gives up. My individual collection of experiences and observations sets me apart from every other writer. My voice is as unique as my thumbprint. For all these reasons, I can win.

~ Insight 29 ~

Build a Wonder of the World

Each writing project is a wonder of the world. I wonder about the world and write. I look at the world with a sense of wonder and write. I hope that my writing encourages readers to wonder about life. I wonder how the world will receive what I've written. It's wondrous to build something concrete out of nothing. It's wonderful when I reach the goal, having constructed the creation as best I can.

The Great Pyramid of Giza is the last remaining wonder of the ancient world. It's made from around 2.3 million stone blocks and took twenty years to build. I heed this remarkable page in history and apply tenacity and vision when I construct my modern day wonders of the world.

I lay one word beside the other, one idea on top of another, one day at a time despite any obstacles and the distance to completion. I go forth in faith and build my writing projects upon the foundation of solid knowledge, step by step, text block by block, with the aim that readers can climb to the peak when I finish.

When I look at the world close up and with a sense of wonder, like Sir David Attenborough, the outlook can permeate my writing and instil wonder in its readers. Writing with childlike wonder is writing as if I'm experiencing something for the first time and this can help produce work that is extra fresh, joyful, and inspiring.

To help me feel a sense of wonder I can ask *what if?* I can lift up my head and observe what lies beyond, behind, or beside my everyday life. I revive the feeling of fascination when I notice nature and absorb my surroundings. I ask people questions about themselves and share experiences. The world becomes wondrous when I take the time to marvel at its beauty, simplicity, complexity, and interconnectedness.

Affirmation

The writing projects I create are modern day wonders of the world in many ways. I imagine the Great Pyramid of Giza and construct a sturdy structure of text, step by step and block by block, until I complete what I envisage.

When I write I'm in the process of manifesting my wonderful dreams. I believe in what I want to achieve. My desire is stable and strong. I expect my dreams to materialise over time as a result of the vision, tenacity, and passion that I place patiently upon the solid foundation of knowledge.

~ Insight 30 ~

What If?

I make it a habit to ask myself *what if?* on a regular basis. *What if?* times often occur during mindless activities because I can think lightly and without restraint. Such times can be conducive to freeing up the imagination and this mind state helps to trigger *what if?* scenarios. For example, every time I go for a walk, wash the car, vacuum, iron, or do gardening I can ask myself *what if?* and have fun with the answers I receive.

What if?s can put a twinkle in my eye. They can cause my mind to take flight and give me light bulb moments. It's useful to have a notepad on hand to jot down any interesting ideas that come to me that could be useful to my writing.

What if?s can get the creative juices flowing in all areas of my life. I can ask myself *what if?* questions about anything: my next project, twists in a plot, unlikely characters in a room together, a different perspective on a topic, my writing dreams, my family members' dreams, walking in someone else's shoes, a bold move, a tactical step, a proposal to put forth, a competition to win, online success, a connection with someone new, a holiday, contributing to a charity, an alternative world, changing my surroundings, and improving my financial position.

What if?s can help to disintegrate writer's block, set me in motion highly charged, and construct an innovative sequence of steps to achieve goals. *What if?s* can help me envisage a way out of a mess and pull me out of predicaments. *What if?s* are fun and they're free. They lighten my vibration and help make me more receptive to the infinite possibilities and ethereal thought energies.

Affirmation

I ask *what if?* about the possibilities for me, my family, my country, and the world. I say *what if?* to help unleash my creativity in writing and in my life. I query *what if?* to invite incredible thoughts that could lead to wondrous creations and clever solutions. *What if?s* enable me to stretch my mind and stamp my dreams on it.

~ Insight 31 ~

Fill Up

Sometimes writing can feel like a bottomless pit. Other times it's a vast blue sky. Either way, writing provides me with infinite room in which to explore, learn, fly, and fall, but it's far from being an empty space. It's a big part of my emotional existence and without it I'd feel like an empty vessel.

Writing fills me with emotions and revelations. It pours dreams, ideas, intrigue, and enthusiasm into me. It's full of questions and challenges. Writing occupies me with puzzles and mind games.

Writing instils an agenda in me. My aspirations fill me with a sense of purpose and direction. Writing supplies me with an ever expanding knowledge base and gratifies me when I complete what I set out to do.

Often what I write fills me with surprise. Reflections may spill out and engulf the page. Writing is daily bread for the soul that fills the spot and nourishes me.

Like my life, my writing is full of chapters yet to be written. Like the universe, writing is an infinite realm full of meaning, substance, and countless worlds that have yet to be found. Like my soul, writing connects me to a divine source, all three of which are limitless.

If ever I feel empty about writing because I have yet to gain the level of public recognition, acknowledgement, and financial return I desire, I remember all the other ways that writing fills me up and see that the cup is half full.

Affirmation

I write because it fills me up. Without writing my head, heart, and soul would have holes in them and I would feel empty. Writing fulfils a creative need in me. It gives me the freedom to fill pages with who I am and what I envisage.

Writing gives me the space and mode of transportation to travel to different places without leaving the room. Writing gives my imagination free rein and an open range in which to soar.

Therefore, my writing cup is already half full and with this outlook I continue to work on becoming a financially sustainable writer to fill the rest of the cup.

~ Insight 32 ~

Lateral Thinking

Edward de Bono's book *Lateral Thinking* is a bestseller about creativity. According to Wikipedia, 'Lateral thinking is solving problems through an indirect and creative approach, using reasoning that is not immediately obvious and involving ideas that may not be obtainable by using only traditional step-by-step logic'. I employ lateral thinking to help me create because linear thinking is generally a succession of predictable, ingrained, tunnel-visioned thoughts.

Lateral thinking is non-critical and non-judgemental. It encourages me to think sideways, upside down, back to front, panoramic, horizontally, and in zig-zags, bringing unexpected and interesting ideas to light. Lateral thinking helps to reveal creative solutions for any challenge. It helps me come up with a fresh approach and a unique perspective.

I refuse to seize the first idea I get to solve a plot problem. I look at ten or more ideas before making a decision on which one to use. I look for the golden thread in a story to follow rather than the common white piece of string. I do this by thinking laterally instead of logically. My subconscious is proficient at using lateral thinking so I let it work on finding uncommon solutions whenever I need to.

Affirmation

I use mind maps, on paper or screen, to explore more than one avenue and to find unusual links between ideas for my writing projects. I brainstorm beyond the box to avoid the obvious and easiest choices.

When I come up with an idea I look east, west, north and south, rather than just straight ahead. I use my peripheral vision when examining an idea to spot a twist or extension of it that may be hovering on the outskirts. I use *what if?s* to help move me into lateral thinking mode. There's always a solution and more than one answer so I take the time to rummage around and find the fresh perspective.

~ Insight 33 ~

Shed Some Gravity

Sometimes I can get too heavy about my writing dreams. I can be too hard on myself. At times I might dread failing to achieve what I envision. My outlook may narrow and I may neglect to balance my life. This type of thinking has the opposite effect of moving me towards my dreams. The frenzied pressure, high anxiety, stern expectations, and work overkill can stunt my progress.

A rigid mind frame restricts me to a boxed-in outlook and a wooden work mode – for example, an *I must succeed* mode or a *time is running out* mode or a *this book's got to be a best seller or else* mode - which can make me feel tired, agitated, and uncreative.

Sometimes I may need to stop and lighten up. I may need to shake off the task master's shackles and feel free again in order to facilitate productive writing. When I shed mental weight I write better because I release my inner child from performing for the authoritative adult in me. My subconscious gains the opportunity to override the critical conscious mind.

Affirmation

I give leave to my inner dictator so that a summer sky may fill my head with light and open space. I release my inner child from labour and feel a joyful weightlessness that defies the gravity I was enduring. Now I move towards my writing dreams with a sense of fun, enthusiasm, and wonder again. Writing is easier and my productivity flows.

~ Insight 34 ~

Hop Around on Lily Pads

I draw a pond of lily pads to explore diverse aspects of a theme and find the golden thread of an idea. By using this method I'm able to turn a simple, common idea into a majestic one that has a powerful perspective. The lily pads can also help to provide me with a rich pitch under ten words that I can use in my submission, online description, or verbal promotion.

First I write a basic idea or theme I want to explore in a circle - or 'lily pad' - in the centre of the page. Then I draw several lily pads around it and connect them with lines to the central lily pad.

My mind hops along the predictable extensions of the central idea and I write each one on a lily pad. I further explore these ideas by connecting more lily pads to them and filling them in with extended developments until I have a whole 'pond' of ideas that trace back to the central theme. I do this until I come across a few developments that are interesting and unusual.

I pick the golden trail of lily pads that turns a common theme into a prince and me into its excited, loyal scribe. I've discovered the kingdom that I'm going to write about.

Affirmation

I use lily pads to explore ideas to find the golden thread that fires my imagination and excites me. The idea that's worth developing usually lies beyond the first ten that appear. This is how I find a new angle, a twist, and a refreshing perspective that sets my story apart although it may be based upon a common theme. Writers have explored all themes. It's up to me to find a new way of presenting them.

~ Insight 35 ~

Fix the Wonky Wheel

Balance is the key to life and *the meaning of life is happiness* are two well-known sayings. Therefore, today I check how much time I give to the six aspects of my life - relationships, health, finances, writing career, spirit, and community - and whether it's balanced.

I can think about how many hours this month I gave to each sector compared to how much time I'd like to have given them. Or I can estimate what percentage of effort I put into every area out of one hundred percent effort.

To help me visualise how balanced my life is I can draw six spokes of a wheel and label each segment with a different aspect of my life. In each respective segment I write in the percentage of time or effort I gave to it this month. Then I mark each percentage level as a line from one side of the segment to the other. Fifty percent would appear as a line from spoke to spoke across the segment, half way down.

When I finish marking a line across each segment the picture of a wheel appears. If it's wonky and would be unable to turn fast in real life I can understand why I may be feeling unbalanced and unhappy.

The wheel indicates which sectors of my life need more, less, or the same attention the following month. Becoming aware of this, I'm able to work on adjusting the wheel so that my life will be better balanced and roll more smoothly. Success in just one sector is unable to provide me with overall joy.

Affirmation

I inspect my life wheel once a month to help keep me on track and more balanced in relation to the amount of energy I give to each sector. I use the wheel as a guide so I can focus on redistributing my time and efforts in a more conscious way, aiming to give each sector the level of input I'd like so as to achieve one hundred percent in all areas. The more even the wheel is the smoother my life will run and the happier I'll feel.

~ Insight 36 ~

New Angles on Old Ideas

I have access to information on writing, the writing industry, and any topic I could think of. The challenge is to blend these resources with my ideas to create a piece of work that will be well received in the market. A way to do this is to employ my unique perspective to create a new angle on what's already out there. I need to present ideas in my own way.

I can approach the search for new angles by juxtaposing unusual plot situations with unlikely characters, reversing character roles in a story, and altering outcomes. I can look at combining two seemingly unrelated topics, amplifying an aspect of a topic, or writing about the topic from another viewpoint to create a new fiction or non-fiction idea.

From a bird's-eye view, all plots and themes are pre-existent creations on which writers continue to build their stories. Ronald Tobias' book *20 Master Plots and How to Build Them* discusses and analyses many common plot structures ranging from 'The Quest' to 'Descension'.

There's a writer's adage that everything has been written before and that there are no new plots, just new twists to them. Every theme has been explored, but there are innumerable ways to demonstrate them through stories. So if I write about what already exists from an unusual outlook I'll create a brand new piece of work that is fresh, exciting, and interesting.

Affirmation

It's unnecessary for me to recreate the plot wheel or invent an original theme to give the reader a new ride. I need fresh angles on old ideas to transport the reader to an exciting, different place.

I find an existing theme that intrigues me. I locate the golden thread, or new angle, amongst the lily pads. Then I develop my story, basing it on the time-tested wheels of the 3 Act Plot Structure. My new angle transforms into a golden carriage that sits upon these wheels and entices the reader aboard. My writing is the horsepower that helps drive the reader to the stimulating, new destination.

I'm open to new angles and use them to give originality to my work. I take what exists already, turn it upside down, and shake it hard to see what falls out of the pockets. I remove the walls dividing preconceived ideas to see if I can merge the ideas into fresh, new perspectives from which to write.

~ Insight 37 ~

Jump Off the Band Wagon

What I decide to write about comes from a place in my heart rather than from what topics and themes are hot in the market right now. I refrain from jumping on the bestseller band wagon because I'm destined to fall off it by the time I finish my book.

Rather than follow fiction and non-fiction fads I listen to my intuition and heed what stirs my passion. Then I rationalise why it's worthy of my and my readers' time. Why should what I have to say be heard? What makes the concept so special?

I'm unable to predict what will be popular in two years' time, but I can write about what I find fascinating or important. Instead of trying to foresee what will win the authors' lotto I think about whether my idea could surprise and exceed a reader's expectations.

If a current popular topic does excite me I give it a different twist or fresh angle to give it legs. I could marry two bestselling book ideas to create an innovative blockbuster. However, I refuse to jump on a theme, topic, or plot bandwagon for the sake of following because publishers and readers love what's innovative. They applaud great surprises and fresh outlooks.

I go with an idea because I have faith in what I envision, not because it's the current trend. This approach has substance and helps me see my project through to completion.

Affirmation

I stay off the book market band wagon and write about those ideas, topics, and themes that make my stomach flutter and my mind whirl. This helps me maintain the level of enthusiasm I need to see a lengthy project through to completion.

I write about what matters to me so that it may matter to others. This approach releases my project from the constraints of conformity, of following to please, and of me racing to finish it before a fad fades.

I avoid following bestseller trends because they're fickle and may be different by the time I finish my book. I refuse to rehash popular plots, characters, and settings because I want to be a trailblazer rather than a trailing author. However, I do explore new concepts that may emerge by turning hot themes and topics on their heads.

~ Insight 38 ~

L.U.C.K.

Labour Under Correct Knowledge

Luck can come when someone who is properly informed strives towards a directly related goal. If I work based on wrong or inaccurate information, I'll fail to get lucky despite the enormous effort I put in. The foundation of knowledge must be solid before I place the ladder to my dreams upon it.

Therefore, before I choose a writing project, I research the market online and on shelf to see what's available from the genre in which I want to write. I speculate as to whether my idea could be a market contender down the track. I check whether any existing books are similar to what I want to write about. If they are, I determine the point of difference with my idea. Is there any room for it alongside what's already available? This helps me set myself up to **L**abour **U**nder **C**orrect **K**nowledge.

Working in a way that's conducive to luck also applies to having correct knowledge of: submission guidelines and criteria, grammar and punctuation rules, genre and word length requirements, what makes writing captivating, and the best way to approach a specific type of writing task. It includes being well informed about the industry and how it works. It's about pinpointing and meeting readers' needs. Luck involves setting the appropriate sale prices for self-publications and understanding publishers' contracts.

Luck can come when I use correct knowledge to my advantage. **L**abouring **U**nder **I**ncorrect **K**nowledge will only bring me L.U.I.K., which is nothing and leads to futility, frustration, wasted effort, and wasted time.

Affirmation

To have any chance of getting a lucky break I must write and get my work out there upon the basis of correct knowledge. I need to have a firm and proper understanding of what I'm going to write, why I'm going to write it, who I'm writing it for, how I'm going to present it in the best way possible, whether there is room for it in the market, when I expect to have it finished, and what price I should sell it at. I need to be well informed about how to promote and get it in front of the right readers.

If I believe my knowledge to be correctly based, then I can cross my fingers for good luck with confidence.

~ Insight 39 ~

Pre-planned Plots

Baby board books have either a very simple plot or no plot. Picture books have a simple plot. Easy readers have a straightforward, yet more involved plot. Chapter books have a main plot and may have one or two subplots. Middle grade books have a few subplots that run alongside the main plot. Both YA books and adult novels need a main plot plus several subplots to support it.

Some writers prefer to plot their novels as they write them. Others need to know where they're headed so they avoid writing themselves into a cage. They prefer to concentrate on the writing as separate from forging the plot. For many writers this is the easiest and most efficient way to approach the intricate task of plotting.

Pre-planned plots provide the writer with the most unobstructed path to follow when writing the first draft because they help cut through the thicket of infinite possibilities beforehand. Plot preparation leads to a clearing in the writer's mind yet still allows lots of opportunity to add spontaneous touches and afterthoughts when writing and editing the drafts.

The main plot is the story line that remains the strongest one all the way through. It's the overarching, largest plot that consists of the overriding dilemma.

The subplots are the smaller dilemmas that offshoot from the main plot. Subplots add layers and intricacies to a story, helping to give it substance and bring it to life. They work around and support the main plot, entwining and merging with it. Every subplot must be so linked to the main plot that the story would fail to function without it.

All plots in the story must follow logically and be a product of the way in which the protagonist handles each obstacle. This creates a character driven story - as opposed to a plot driven action story like in an action movie - and therefore elicits a strong emotional response from the reader, creating a deeper connection.

Affirmation

I plot and subplot according to my story's readership requirements. I prepare a blueprint for the main plot in bullet point form under the 3 Act Structure. Then I do the same for any subplots and add them beneath the list of the main plot's points.

I give each individual plot its own colour code for easy identification. This blueprint prepares me for my plot tree or chapter summaries to which I will transfer the colour coded plots points and flesh them out in more detail with actual scenes.

~ Insight 40 ~

Family and Friends Follow My Lead

My family and friends treat my writing with as much respect as I do. If I tell them that I need to write for an hour today, they'll manage to work my unavailability into their plans. If I make it known that I have to write for a long period because I have a deadline to meet, they'll do their best to accommodate my need for space and quiet.

If I'm coy about my writing needs or help everyone yet fail to write, the people around me will regard my writing time as unimportant. If writing is last on my list, how can I expect others to give it priority? If I disguise my plans to write with an urgent duty I need to perform, I'm being dishonest and believe that others are unable to respect my writing commitments.

If there are young children in my care I write when they're asleep. Or I can ask a friend or family member to mind my children for half an hour if I need a break to write. I ask for assistance because attending to my writing dreams helps keep me balanced and this benefits all those around me.

When I respect my writing enough to give it space in my day and I behave like writing matters, my family and friends take an interest. If I demonstrate commitment to my writing, they'll sense the importance of it and will learn to take it seriously too. When I'm honest and clear about my writing intentions I show regard for my dreams. Family and friends will then follow my lead, working in with my writing needs as best they can.

Affirmation

Respect for my writing starts with me. Therefore, I let my family and friends know when I need to write. I ask them for some time and quiet or advise them that I have to remove myself to write for a set period. I place importance on my writing time and am keen to show them what writing means to me. My family and friends love me and, following my lead, they'll come to regard my writing needs as important too.

~ Insight 41 ~

Act Up

To pre-plan an emotionally powerful story, I construct a plot summary blueprint in bullet point form under the 3

Act Structure. In other words, work out the story's beginning, middle and end. Aristotle, born 384 BC, designed this 3 Act Structure framework upon which fiction writers have built their stories for centuries.

Act 1 is the beginning. It sets up the protagonist's problems. The problems must push the main character to fix them because there's a lot at stake. The subplots must impose some smaller difficulties on the protagonist that arise from the main plot.

Act 2 is the middle where the rising action occurs. The main character's obstacles become increasingly difficult to overcome to the point that solutions seem unlikely. The worsening situation occurs as a direct result of the main character's attempts to defeat the preceding challenges. The reader must feel that all hope is lost at the end of Act 2.

Act 3 contains the end of the story. It provides the solutions to the problems that climaxed at the end of Act 2. The protagonist must work out the solutions to each problem based on his or her own merits.

In summary, I dump all the crises from the main plot and subplots on my protagonist in Act 1. In Act 2 I increase the difficulty and reduce the likelihood of the protagonist fixing the crises so that the predicament peaks. In Act 3 my protagonist resolves all the crises in an unexpected way, creating an intriguing twist that's character driven.

Affirmation

I create a basic plot summary blueprint of my main plot and individual subplots in bullet point form, stacking them under the headings Act 1, Act 2 and Act 3 and colour coding each plot. Then I ensure that every plot has a satisfying beginning, middle, and end.

I make the protagonist resolve the peaking catastrophes in Act 3 using his or her own initiative, growth, actions, strengths, and personality in order to emotionally satisfy the reader. I resolve the story in this way to allow the reader the opportunity to predict how the protagonist might overcome the seemingly impossible situations and to accept a logical conclusion that was unforeseen.

An interesting character driven main plot, supported by well woven subplots within a strong 3 Act Structure, helps to make my story hard to put down.

~ Insight 42 ~

Escape and Survival

Readers want to learn about the survival of my protagonist in adverse conditions to escape their own lives for a while. Readers want to find out how a character's thought processes and logic get him or her out of a calamitous, hopeless situation resulting in triumph over the antagonist. The antagonist could be a person, a group of people, an institution, the protagonist's inner self, the weather, or some other threatening situation.

My stories need to be about purposeful human beings winning against setbacks on their own merits. Lucky circumstances that save the day, or secondary characters that solve the main character's problems, or God's holy intervention that miraculously fixes everything, disappoints and dismays the reader. Rather, the reader wants to witness how my protagonist's courage, motivation, genius, and strength came to the rescue.

Readers struggle in their own lives to survive every day. A reader can gain relief from this by living fresh experiences and feelings through a remarkable character. Just as a fan barracks for a football team and feels the victories and failures with the team, so too the reader lives vicariously through the character.

And it's got to be a good game all the way to win the reader over.

Affirmation

I'm mindful that the reader wants to escape through my protagonist. The harder my main character works to survive the plot, the greater the chance of survival in the reader's memory and heart.

I create a protagonist with purpose to whom the reader wants to relate. Then I design a plot of mounting obstacles that logically link to each other and to the protagonist's personal responses to each obstacle. I'm careful that these responses reflect the protagonist's character, traits, and history.

I ensure the protagonist is the saviour, the one who finds the solution and ultimately conducts the rescue. By doing this, I provide the reader with the greatest escape.

~ Insight 43 ~

Plot Trees

My colour coded plot summary blueprint under the 3 Act Structure will help me construct a plot tree or write chapter summaries in which I will nominate the actual scenes of the story. To sequence the story's scenes in a very visual and workable way I can use a plot tree, which is a treelike structure on paper, along with coloured pencils. Butcher paper is a great size to work with. Alternatively, I can choose to use one of the story plotting programs available online.

Plotting on paper, I start from the top of the page and construct a vertical trunk of connecting boxes each of which contain a progressive main plot point belonging to Act 1 with the end point of Act 1 in the bottom box.

From the first plot point box I sprout branches of boxes containing possible scenes for it. I do this for the rest of the plot boxes. Then I erase, replace, and rearrange the scenes until the sequence seems like a strong, sturdy trunk.

I refer again to my colour coded plot summary blueprint and use it as a guide. One subplot at a time, in its designated colour code, I sprout boxes from the main scenes. In them I write potential subplot scenes that could work in with or alongside the main scene. This is how I entwine the subplots around and into the main plot. The different colours help me identify the unfolding of each subplot, enabling me to adjust the pacing if need be.

A subplot can appear intermittently down the trunk of the main plot because it's a secondary story. However, each subplot must support the main plot to the point that if I removed it from the tree the main story would fall down.

When I finish Act 1 I move onto Act 2 using the same method as described. Then I complete Act 3. Act 2 is the longest act. Act 1 tends to be the shortest, but it can be about as long as Act 3 in some cases. I headline the beginnings of Acts 1, 2, and 3 beside the tree trunk for easy navigation.

As the branches of scenes grow and the plot tree thickens I create a magic, faraway tree that will take the reader where I want him or her to go.

Affirmation

My story starts as a bare tree trunk of main plot points. I connect branches of possible scenes to them and choose the best arrangement to create the best sequence of scenes. Then I wind vines of subplot scenes around the main trunk and merge any scenes that I can.

I colour code all scenes to keep track of each subplot's prevalence and distribution throughout the plot tree. This helps me to have balance and good pacing throughout the story.

I ensure that every subplot serves to make the story work. I test this by mentally removing subplot scenes to see whether the main plot would collapse without them. If the main plot holds up without the subplot, I fasten the loose subplot tighter to the main plot so that the story relies on it to function.

~ Insight 44 ~

Duty of Care to Characters

I take great care of my characters. I refrain from forcing them to do anything that goes against their constitution. They have the right to oppose what I've plotted for them. I get to know my characters better as my manuscript develops so if I come to discover that what I've written is out of line with who they are I heed the objections they raise in my mind.

I create my characters in detail and understand them as best I can before I design their story. This helps to facilitate a rich character driven plot that appeals to fiction readers wanting a moving story to which they can connect.

I care for my characters by keeping them consistent and well defined throughout the manuscript.

To assist me I jot down who each character is and what they look like on cue cards and refer to the cards as I write. With every draft I refine and sharpen my characters' responses, perceptions, and dialogue congruous to the type of people they are, their agendas, and the crosses they bear.

Each draft brings me closer to transmitting the characters' feelings with transparency and truth. With enough drafts the characters will seem like their own bona fide entities in charge of their own destinies and dependent upon the choices they make.

If a character's decision fails to ring true I change the response and adjust the next plot point that relied on that decision. I'm mindful of my characters' attributes, beliefs, motivations, pasts, and personalities, which all help to determine the ensuing plot points and move the story forwards.

Affirmation

I'm keeper of my characters. I have a duty of care to them. Therefore, I refuse to push and pull my characters around like hostages held at gunpoint to make the original plot plan work. With each draft I tinker and tweak the plot, ensuring that it fits snugly around the natural behaviour of the characters and that the sequence of unfolding events is dependent upon their genuine personal influences.

~ Insight 45 ~

Draw the Lines

Deadlines are crucial to my writing success. If I decide to create a piece of work to submit to publishers or competitions the deadline works on me like a faithful winch hauling me towards completion. I take on the deadline full heartedly and give my writing project all I've got until the end.

Although an imminent deadline pressures me, I love that it compelled me to plan how to get the job done over a set time period. I enjoy how it activates me and commits me to a project. I like how a deadline prompts me to do what it takes on a daily basis, treat my writing like a business, craft my work in a methodical way, finish the project in a timely manner, and meet the set criteria as a professional writer would.

Cut-off dates give me a sense of direction and purpose. They pose a healthy challenge and help shape my writing life. Although stretching to meet deadlines can be uncomfortable, ultimately it feels good. It's okay to feel the stress that time limits can rouse. This stress is productive and helps to discipline me.

Deadlines fill me with satisfaction when I deliver and they teach me how to better organise myself if I fail to meet them. Deadlines are treasured time keepers that draw a daily response from me and urge me to keep the goals I set for myself. Deadlines push me towards my dreams.

Affirmation

Deadlines stretch me and help keep my writing life in shape. Time targets keep me on my toes and reaching for the stars. They increase my activity towards my dreams and support me along my writing journey.

I honour deadlines whether they be self-made or from an external source. I treat deadlines with the utmost respect and fulfil them to the best of my ability because deadlines are lifelines to my writing success.

~ Insight 46 ~

Write in the Dark

Sometimes I can get lost in the dark with writing. The path can become obscure. However, there's reassurance in knowing that it's okay to feel my way along until I can see where I'm going again. I can go a step further and use the light that shines from my heart to help show me the way forwards.

My heart light is a torch that can illuminate life's meanings, lessons, and connections. It can shed light on the past, present, and future. It can help me find the glinting jewels in dimly lit ideas, grey areas, and labyrinthine possibilities. My heart can reveal the golden crux of the matter.

I venture forth knowing that there's always a light at the end of the tunnel. I may not see a way out for my characters right now, but I know it's there. It's always there. To help myself find it I hold up my torch and hunt around without tunnel vision meaning without wearing 'horse blinkers' that pre-empt or exclude.

Sometimes when I write I enter dark areas of my mind: the chambers of sad memories, the caves of my suppressed feelings, and the dungeons where the chains of entangled conflicts lie. I can use what I find in the dark to create powerful plot points and heart-wrenching character responses. Solutions to plot challenges tend to glow in this gloom.

Sometimes when I write I encounter shady parts of me in dark alleyways or confront strange parts that make me uneasy and ashamed. Excellent. Readers tend to love writers who immerse them in this kind of darkness.

Bryce Courtenay compared writing a finished novel to living for a year in the dark. Authors tend to discover whether their end products shine when they emerge from the tunnel and hold their books up to the light. All writers including bestselling authors spend time in the dark in various ways. Therefore, I can expect to. It's an inescapable part of the writer's journey.

Affirmation

I'm unafraid of writing in the dark. Many forms of darkness assist my writing. I find blessings in the blackness and solutions in the shadows.

The darkness helps me retrieve glinting ideas from unforeseen places. It gives my writing depth, reality, and intrigue. It can help to create the big scenes in my story.

Also, the contrast enables me to appreciate the light when I break through. Throughout my writing journey I use all types of darkness to light up the way.

~ Insight 47 ~

Go to the Inner Sanctuary

Often at the end of Pilates, Yoga, and Body Balance classes there's a ten minute meditation session to clear and settle the mind after balancing the body. I can enjoy similar short meditation sessions at home to help quieten my conscious mind in preparation for writing.

I lie down in a comfortable position with palms facing upwards. I urge my mind to let go and envision handing my cares over to the universe. I focus on breathing in through the nose and out through the mouth, expanding and contracting my ribs widthways rather than heaving up and down which makes my ribs pop up. Breathing wide is how a baby breathes and it allows me to use much more of my lungs so that I inhale increased oxygen and expel more carbon dioxide.

I tell individual parts of my body to relax, starting from my toes and working up to my head. I meld into what I'm lying upon. I feel weightless and mind travel to the special place that I have chosen to be my sanctuary.

I picture my sanctuary clearly. It fills me with serenity and happiness. I could be on top of a mountain surrounded by clouds and light, or perhaps in an ice wonderland, or in a perfect forest clearing, or up in space gazing at beautiful blue Earth. My sanctuary helps neutralise my thoughts, preparing me to write with clarity, calmness, and confidence.

Affirmation

I use short meditation periods to help prepare my head, heart, and soul to write. I relax my mind and body to change my vibration to a frequency that helps to facilitate the best writing. I detach myself from what's going on around me to write from a clear, calm place. I go to my sanctuary whenever I need to restore peace, see beauty, and feel safe.

~ Insight 48 ~

Get Down

It's considered common knowledge that editing is eighty percent of the work required to complete a publishable project. Therefore, a wise approach is to get down the entire first draft in preparation for the longer editing stage and the project's completion.

If I aim to complete a novel's first draft in a relatively short time, meaning weeks or months, my expectations of moving past the first draft tend to remain strong because I can see beyond it to the editing stage.

This vision helps me feel like I'm in transit on a direct course and that I'll be arriving at the next phase soon. The anticipation boosts my morale and motivates me. It strengthens the habit to finish what I start and helps keep my work content consistent. Therefore, I resist the urge to slow down and perfect the early pages before I finish the entire first draft.

Also, it's unproductive and deflating to waste words I've laboured over due to premature editing. I want to avoid discarding perfection to save time and energy.

After I get the first draft down I may find that the first chapters need to change. I may have to adjust major sections or rearrange the sequence of events to improve the overall delivery. I might realise after reviewing the first draft that I need to change the point of view, remove or add elements to the plot, and re-word information in the first chapters due to the great angle that developed in the middle chapters. I may realise that parts of the beginning have become irrelevant and unnecessary.

To make the editing stage easier, I can be mindful of shielding the first draft from basic writing weaknesses. For example, I can avoid using adverbs that clutter like *just, actually, really, very, basically,* and vague words like *nice, it, special,* and *that.*

I can refrain from writing cumbersome phrases like *try to, begin to,* and using dangling modifiers and *ing* participles. I can steer clear of descriptive narrative words like *thought, felt, decided, realised,* and of naming emotions which indicate telling rather than showing the story. I can become proficient at writing first drafts in the active voice instead of the passive. I can write without using doubling-up phrases like *return back.*

The more I recognise the basic flaws as I write them, the better I'll become at omitting them from the first draft automatically. This aside, my first draft will still be as rough as guts or resemble a dog's breakfast. That's okay because the focus was on finishing it and now I'm ready to begin the refinement process called editing.

Affirmation

I refuse to let the first chapter captivate and detain me for editing because this would elongate the first draft tunnel, waste edited words, and endanger the project's completion. I stick to my daily word count and maintain momentum to get the book's first draft down in weeks as opposed to years.

To help reduce the editing workload I become natural at using efficient words to complete the first draft. I get the first draft over and done with fast so I can move on to editing it into a publishable form.

~ Insight 49 ~

Heed the Rules

I adhere to all submission rules. I re-read them several times to ensure I give my proposal or entry a chance to be accepted. I check my final application to confirm that I have followed the correct format and met all criteria. If I overlook any part of this process I'll sabotage the prospect of success before I send off my work.

I keep within the word counts that apply to different genres, readership age groups, publishers' preferences, and competitions. I identify suitable themes or topics. I abide by the text formatting and page layout requirements. I use the spelling and grammar checker, but always proof read my work to pick up any errors the program may overlook. I send off my work in accordance with the options I'm given using the correct payment method, if applicable.

I learn about appropriate word usage for my particular readership. I find out the word difficulty level I should employ. I choose whether to use contractions or full phrases and stay consistent with this decision throughout the piece. I'm careful to omit slang in narrative or formal passages. I avoid using academic writing in casual pieces.

However, I get down the first draft without focussing on the rules. It's important to write the first draft freely without applying the mental park brake of regulations so that the stream of consciousness flows and I transfer complete thoughts into words. Of course, the better I'm able to spontaneously write heeding some rules the less editing work the subsequent drafts will need and the more time I'll save.

As an aspiring writer it's safer to comply with the grammar, spelling, and punctuation rules in the final draft. It's in my best interests to follow genre and readership guidelines and stay within the boundaries. However, as a seasoned writer with expertise, I may choose to bend or break certain rules skilfully to produce effects that work well.

Affirmation

I obey all submission and industry rules to give myself the best chance of acceptance and to avoid wasting time and money.

I write my first draft without focussing on correct grammar, punctuation, and spelling to encourage my creativity to flow freely rather than be self-conscious. This way, I'm able to connect to the sub-conscious source that offers deeper wisdom and wider perspective. However, the more natural I become at writing using the basic rules the less editing work I'll need to do.

I refrain from flouting some of the writing regulations until I become an established, experienced writer because this is the more dependable road to professional success. For now I work within the boundaries knowing that in due course I'll acquire the expertise to cross them with confidence and craftsmanship.

~ Insight 50 ~

Get On With It

Procrastination with writing stems from the fear that I might fail to meet my expectations and fulfil my dreams. This is an understandable reaction, but it's unacceptable. I see procrastination for what it is: fear driven behaviour.

Fear or faith can steer my outlook and drive my actions. Fear and faith produce very different results. Fear and faith affect my head, heart, and soul in opposite ways. Therefore, I choose faith because it's the kinder, more rewarding approach to life. Faith gives me a happier experience. So in faith I get on with writing.

I learn to identify any attempt I make to procrastinate. I shove the non-productive urge back in its box and tell it where to go because fear fades when I face it.

It's unthinkable to wonder what might have been if I had've had the courage to write and go for my dreams. Writing is a top priority and whenever I give it the attention it deserves I feel content, just like I do when I attend to other priorities.

It's okay if I only get down half of the writing I hoped to in a sitting because I've also made mental progress that I'm unable to see on the page or screen yet. I've engaged in thought processes along with the act of writing. My subconscious has contemplated idea arrangements and juxtapositions. Words will be forthcoming when I sit down to write again.

The more I ignore procrastination the happier, more energetic, and lighter I feel. It becomes easier to write because action is the habit rather than procrastination. Over time, habits make or break me so I guard against procrastination at every turn.

Affirmation

I choose to approach life with the outlook of faith. I do this to have a better life experience and remain in pursuit of my dreams. Action is my habit. My writing dreams are the agenda. Faith is my friend.

~ Insight 51 ~

Character Cards

It can be a challenge to keep recalling a character's appearance and traits especially if it's a secondary character or if I've made attribute changes. Character cards can help me get the first draft down in a more efficient, error free manner so it's a good idea to keep character cards beside me as I work.

I follow the plot tree or chapter summary to write my first draft, but can use cards as the tool to keep me consistent with my characters. The card information can contain a character's name, appearance, age, qualities, vices, pet sayings, fears, idiosyncrasies, hates and so on. I do this for every character, even the peripheral ones, so that when I write them into the story I depict them in a uniform way. For example, I ensure that a character's eye colour remains the same throughout.

I may need to change a character's attributes during the course of getting the story down, so I alter the character cards as I go to keep up with the adjustments. I can use the amended cards to fix the manuscript before the point of change and update the character's depiction, but it may be easier to complete the first draft and make any adjustments during the second draft edit.

Using character cards saves me time and head space. They help me move my book into the top one percent by bringing it closer to perfection and professionalism. Character inconsistency is a common writing faux pas that is ghastly to editors and readers.

Affirmation

I make character cards because they save me time and effort in the long run. I do myself a favour and rely on the cards rather than on my memory to help me get down characters in the first draft with a degree of consistency. It's too much to expect myself to remember everything about my characters especially if I make changes to their attributes along the way.

I work smart by referring to character cards. They help me create a professional product that meets the reader's expectations.

~ Insight 52 ~

Hold Onto the Dream

Many authors dream of making a good living from writing, however the 2014 Digital Book World and Writer's Digest Author Survey found that most traditional and self-published authors struggle to do this. Out of 9,210 surveyed writers '...54% of traditionally-published authors and almost 80% of go-it-alone writers are making less than $1,000 (£600) a year.' These statistics are surprising, but they fail to unnerve me.

Firstly, I draw great strength in knowing that I was born to write and that I'll continue to write for the rest of my life. Secondly, sources such as www.easywaytowrite.com advise that the writers who refuse to quit despite the setbacks and those who write at least two thousand words a day are the ones likely to become financially sustainable career writers.

Therefore, I accept that to become a viable full time writer my daily word count must be at least two thousand and that I need to soldier on in all circumstances. I also acknowledge that I may have to write a variety of material to create a regular income from writing.

I hold onto my dreams with an understanding of the daily commitment they require from me to uphold them. I hold onto my dreams with the view of enjoying the adventure. I persist and persevere using a reliable work ethic despite how distant becoming a full time, profitable writer may seem sometimes.

Rewards for my efforts may come sooner than I expect. Commercial success could be waiting for me around the next career corner. My next publication could gain popularity and help launch me into the professional writer's life. I refuse to give in to the unknown because who knows what's in store?

Affirmation

I hold onto my writing dreams under all circumstances and always with the view that they're possible. I refuse to give in. I refuse to rest on my laurels. I keep writing, editing, submitting, self-publishing, and learning about the craft and industry to help grant me the opportunity to become a writer with a sustainable career. The quicker I begin writing two thousand words a day, the faster my dreams are likely to materialise.

~ Insight 53 ~

Done and Dusted

I'm in the minority of writers that follows through and does what it takes to complete projects. Most writers start manuscripts they never finish. Often this occurs because they edit the first chapters, research, and plot to no end, but I'm different.

I put time and effort into creating an exciting, workable plot plan, but refuse to plot indefinitely. I tinker with the plot after I read the finished first draft. I only conduct the basic research I need to get the first draft done. I save editing for the start of the second draft. With these approaches I could write a first draft novel in thirty to sixty days.

I use momentum to get the first draft done and dusted fast. This way my enthusiasm stays strong, I stay connected throughout the exercise, I delight in the progress, and enjoy the feeling of accomplishment upon completion.

I always finish what I start because it's too easy to give up and waste the road thus travelled. A track record of discarded writing pieces keeps me out of the game mentally and removes any chance of market success. I refuse to have a drawer of semi-loved creations, dusty ideas, or computer files of abandoned efforts.

I can only know what it takes to write a book if I complete one and experience the entire creative process. I can only call myself a book author when my book has a beginning, middle, and end. I can only submit confidently if I finish the piece and polish it to the best of my ability.

Affirmation

I contain my plotting and research to get the first draft done and dusted. I begin to edit and conduct deeper research on the second draft.

I'm a writer who completes projects. Finishing what I start is paramount to my writing success. The momentum I create helps to keep me enthusiastic and consistent. The progress I make supports my self-esteem and vision. My writing projects can count on me.

~ Insight 54 ~

What's It Worth?

My talent and passion for writing is worthy of investment. It's okay to spend time and money on writing courses, resources, writers' events, self-help e-books, maintaining a positive attitude, website creation, and book assessments. It's worth taking the time to practise writing. Any investment I make in self-development is worthwhile if I put what I learn to use.

Sometimes I may wonder whether my writing is good enough to involve other people to help improve it. Sometimes I may think it's unnecessary for my work to undergo external evaluation. However, it's valuable to identify my writing's strengths and weaknesses in order to progress. Fresh eyes and expert advice will draw my attention to faulty areas of my work that need fixing.

Sometimes I may feel like I'm wasting my time writing with little reward to show for it so far. However, investing time and energy into goals and dreams is a worthy cause in itself. People need hope and dreams to survive and these driving mechanisms are paramount to achieving success. It's also worth writing to fulfil a natural need in me and to be able to honestly call myself a writer.

It's worth investing time into sharpening my skills and putting into practice what I learn about the nuts and bolts of writing just to become a better writer.

It's worth taking the time to evaluate whether my writing has communicated what I intended simply to become a better communicator. Therefore, any gain beyond this is well worth the time and effort.

Affirmation

The time I invest in writing pleases my higher self. The money I spend on learning to write well for the market is money spent wisely when I apply the knowledge. I may feel awkward at times exposing myself to feedback, but my writing progress is worth it.

I invest time and money in my development and my dreams because doing so reinforces my conviction to succeed.

In conclusion, my writing is worthy.

~ Insight 55 ~

Invite Paul the Venetian Master

I call upon Ascended Master Paul the Venetian to help me with my writing. I invite him to surround me with his divine loving vibration. I request his assistance to open up the channels of higher intellect and deeper emotions in me so they may flow out through my fingertips and into my words.

I ask the Venetian Master to bless me with articulate self-expression so I may convey meanings with clarity and insight. I request that he help me communicate feelings with truth and transparency.

I tune into Master Paul and ask him to bestow upon me a humble sense of knowingness and intuition that allows me to impart formal and informal knowledge with the intent of serving others.

I request that the Ascended Master help me keep my ego in check when I write in order to deliver the purest, least self-conscious writing possible.

Affirmation

Before I write I surround myself with the golden pink rays of divine love that come from Paul the Venetian. His compassion, patience, and understanding calm me. I feel my heart open up to the intuitive and creative energies to which he is devoted. I trust in my higher self to deliver wisdom through my words. I thank the Master for his divine presence and attention.

~ Insight 56 ~

Basic Instructions for a Sweet Ride

According to the online Urban Dictionary, a sweet ride is 'an automobile or otherwise that is worthy of praise. The experience found when cruising in said vehicle is extremely pleasurable and braggable'.

There are several fundamental features that I'd be wise to install in my story to provide a reliable base vehicle that can offer the reader a sweet ride:

- I write what I know best,
- My characters are believable and behave believably,
- I challenge my main character with serious conflict that requires resolution,
- My protagonist keeps pushing against the conflict and grows by doing so, thereby becoming an improved character by the story's end,
- The antagonist's threat reveals my main character's strength,
- I show, instead of tell, the story at least eighty percent of the time,
- I avoid lists that describe my characters and surroundings,
- Every character must have a purpose,

- Every plot event must be necessary to the story's unfolding,
- I choose names of places and people carefully because they affect the reader's experience,
- I excite the reader by throwing imaginative, active characters into a fresh plot with a twist.

Affirmation

Before I invite any reader to climb aboard and strap into my story, I install the several basic standard features. Having done this, I can then look at adding high quality accessories and touches to my manuscript - such as an opening sentence purely about story and cliff-hanger chapter endings – which will help upgrade my basic sweet ride to a ripper read.

~ Insight 57 ~

Network with an Open Heart

I welcome other writers into my life. We are of similar ilk and can relate to the challenges and joys we experience on the writer's journey. We can provide company to each other along the way and offer mutual support and validation.

Networking with other writers and writing groups is important to my growth because it gives me a sounding board, helps me feel connected, announces to the universe that I'm a writer, gets me used to making my work public, and helps to break down any apprehension I may have of sharing my work. There's room for all of us because we are unique individuals.

I learn how to verbally express my writing experiences. The more I share them with other writers the more eloquent and comfortable I'll feel doing so.

I value the importance of having a website/blog to plug into the writing industry network so that it can easily access me, check me out, and interact with me. I'm open to using the internet to build connections with writers, readers, publishers, and writers' organisations.

Affirmation

I network with an open heart. I allow writers into my world and draw strength from them. I share what I know with others and am open to receive what they offer with me. Together we can soften writing's solitary nature and help each other through challenges.

I use the internet to network and help me establish my place in the writing industry. I have no qualms about promoting myself and my writing through networks.

~ Insight 58 ~

Put On a Show

Showing a story rather than telling it is a crucial element of excellent fiction writing. This writing technique helps to bring my words and characters to life. It instils a strong sense of realness. Showing a story helps to pull readers in by their senses and emotions. It serves to immerse them in the world I have created.

It's imperative to show a story to enable the reader to become intimate, hold interest, and fall into the fictive dream. This method also allows me to build suspense by not spelling out situations, which encourages the reader to develop conclusions and make predictions.

To show not tell I avoid long passages of narrative description that reads as a list of details. I refrain from using nouns to describe emotions. Instead, I demonstrate characters and their feelings through actions, speech, facial expressions, observations, and body language. This also helps to suggest what the characters are experiencing internally rather than telling the reader outright.

I describe the setting, the past, relationships, and appearances by scattering specific choice words throughout the text including the dialogue. I employ the characters' observations to reveal descriptive details in a subtle way.

I use words other than *he said* to help show a character's disposition, but I keep these substitutes simple so as to draw minimal attention to them and keep the reader in the fictive dream. For example, I write *he whispered*, but avoid using pompous or self-conscious expressions like *he ejaculated*.

I'm always mindful of showing rather than telling a story so I can offer the reader an effective reading experience. I do my best to put on a great show every time. The reader deserves it.

Affirmation

I'm a story shower rather than a story teller. I avoid using long passages of narrative description to depict characters, emotions, history, relationships, and settings. I camouflage descriptions and create suggestions amidst the characters' dialogue, facial expressions, actions, experiences, and observations. I use the senses to convey emotions rather than the nouns.

I show instead of tell to give readers an intimate, realistic, satisfying performance and to draw out emotional responses from them.

~ Insight 59 ~

Chances Are

Whenever I take steps towards my writing dreams I signal to the universe that I own the dreams and that they're mine to attain. The universe knows that I'm giving to my dreams in order to receive them. It recognises that I'm showing faith and rejecting doubt, demonstrating courage and rejecting fear. This is what the universe wants me to do. This is the outlook that life encourages so that it can continue. The universe responds to my affirmative actions by setting wheels in motion somewhere to assist me.

When I take chances and move towards a dream with high energy and good intent, the universe senses the positive action and may reciprocate. Even if I'm unable to see its response I can already feel the enthusiasm and excitement that's manifesting in and around me. The universe works in ways greater than I understand and I trust it to offer me opportunities and support.

Affirmation

I visualise my writing dreams and make confident moves to achieve them based on correct knowledge. The universe is made of energy and so responds to my energy. Therefore, I take steps towards my dreams with faith and the belief that the universe is there to help me manifest them in all sorts of ways. Chances are that the wheels are already in motion and my dreams are on their way.

~ Insight 60 ~

How to Tell

Telling, as opposed to showing, is the descriptive narrative method I use when I want to convey information to the reader in a direct, fast, and rather clinical way. Therefore, I limit the telling technique to twenty percent of my fictional prose since my story's goal is to emotionally connect with the reader.

I use telling when it's less important for the reader to empathise with my characters. Telling can be an effective way to change the story pace and get information across provided I'm mindful that the more telling I do the more emotionally detached the reader will become. Whenever I list descriptive details in a story I give it a non-fiction feel.

The fiction genre types that use more of the telling method include fantasy fiction and science fiction because they need to explain to the reader how technical matters and alternative worlds work. Police and news reports and academic essays tell us about real events and information rather than show us through suggestion.

To tell instead of show I use the names of emotions instead of conveying them through a character's facial expressions, dialogue, perceptions, and actions. I use direct descriptions to relay settings and appearances rather than place choice words throughout the text. I inform the reader of the subject's history, background, and relationships in direct blocks of prose, rather than reveal these details discreetly. The telling technique is better suited to non-fiction pieces.

Affirmation

I have a clear understanding of when to use tell rather than show in my work. I use the telling technique sparingly in fiction so that I keep the reader drawn in and emotionally attached to my story. I save long blocks of narrative description for fantasy and science fiction when the reader requires explanations as to how the mechanics of a world work.

I use rationed portions of telling to help vary the pace of my fiction story, but I use the show approach at least eighty percent of the time.

~ Insight 61 ~

Purge the Passive

I'm an active writer. I write in the active voice. I refuse to let the subjects in my sentences be the victims of passive verb constructs. My subjects' actions are assertive.

I'm always on the lookout for passive writing that skulks and sneaks its way onto the page. It tries to hide right under my nose by cringing in the nooks between brave, strong phrases. For example, if I write *the man was bitten by the dog* I immediately pounce on the passive phrase and change it to *the dog bit the man*. With active writing I empower the dog which did the biting action. The man is the object of the dog's bite, but in the passive voice he became the subject doing the action of receiving the dog's bite.

The passive voice creates wordy writing that is indirect and weak. I make it my business to practise writing in the active voice so I can cut out unnecessary words, better execute the first draft, and save a lot of editing time later.

There are times when it can be useful to write in the passive voice, but these are infrequent. One time is when a writer wants to conceal who did the action from the reader on purpose, such as *the bell was rung on the night of her death*. The writer keeps the identity of who rang the bell a mystery.

Another time to use passive writing is when the writer is unaware of who did an action, such as a lawyer in a court case, and the passive phrase is practical. For example, *the cake was eaten at three o'clock* is a practical phrase if no-one actually knew who ate the cake. The active voice could read as *Mrs Brown ate the cake at three o'clock*.

A staunch stance against passive writing strengthens my characters' presence, my sentence structure, and style. An active voice empowers my writing by giving it volume, pace, and directness. It gets rid of unnecessary words. Active verbs instil energy in the reader and also conserve it by providing a clear, uncluttered transmittance of the meaning I wish to convey.

Affirmation

My characters and sentence subjects are strong. They assert their actions and wills rather than let the objects of their actions become the sentence subjects.

When I write using the passive voice my prose becomes wordy, haughty, and flimsy. Therefore, unless I use passive writing for a special purpose, it has no place in my solid, straight sentence structure.

The more conscious I become of writing passive phrases the more efficient I become at eliminating their weakness from my work at the outset, saving me hours of editing. However, I continue to hunt down sneaky passive writing throughout the editing process because it can be easy to overlook.

~ Insight 62 ~

Send the Strongest Signals

There are many ways to convey to the universe that I own my dreams and intend to fulfil them. There are many positive actions I can take to demonstrate that I want to work with the universe to attain them. There are lots of ways to show I'm willing to take chances and invest my energy in the faith that the universe will favour and support me.

Some positive actions may include: researching, learning about writing, nutting out projects, saying affirmations, arranging non-fiction interviews, sending query letters, requesting information and reports to collect facts for a project, learning how to use technology to my writing advantage, having my work edited or assessed, and so on.

However, the strongest signals I transmit to the universe tend to occur when I'm writing, self-editing, and getting my work out there. These actions confirm in the most physical way that the writing dreams are mine and that I'm backing the chance I'll achieve them.

When I infuse positive actions towards a dream with enthusiasm I further strengthen the signals I send to the universe. The word *enthusiasm* comes from the Greek word 'entheos' meaning 'having the god within'.

In archaic English *enthusiasm* means 'ecstasy arising from supposed possession of a god'. A more modern meaning is 'rapturous inspiration like that caused by a god'.

Today people are enthusiastic about anything and we can take *enthusiasm* to mean a great keenness and excitement that feels as if we are inspired and plugged in to the universe's positive energy.

Affirmation

I take chances and make moves towards my writing dreams believing that the universe senses my energy and wants to support my good intentions. I infuse positive actions with enthusiasm to emit stronger signals. I have faith that somewhere, somehow, the universe is responding to my vibrations and that the delivery of my dreams is on the way.

~ Insight 63 ~

Write in Multi-dimensional Form

In my writing I use the five physical senses - sight, sound, touch, taste, and smell - to help evoke a realistic experience in the reader. I use my sixth sense to guide me. When I employ all these senses I add dimension to my prose that enables my story to jump out and interact with the reader.

There are other ways I can prise flat words off the page. These include showing the story instead of telling it and using active rather than passive sentences. Braiding subplots into the main plot serves to multi-level the story and multi-layer the meanings, adding depth and complexity.

I also heed Shakespeare's statement *brevity is the soul of wit and tediousness the limbs and outward flourishes*, which I can take to mean that my writing becomes more exciting and has more impact when I remove extraneous matter such as floral sentences and pompous words.

My writing can seem to float if it's consistent, error free, and unambiguous. Easy, stumble-free reading helps lift the reader up and away.

I do my best to make my characters appear three dimensional. Besides experiencing life through the full range of sensory perceptions, they need to have layered personalities to seem authentic. This enables them to reach out and touch the reader.

My story rises from the page and hovers if it succeeds in suspending the reader in a fictive spell throughout the entire piece. To help me achieve this I keep my presence right out of the picture, but subtly convey my experiences, thoughts, and feelings through wholehearted characters.

Affirmation

I give my story height, width, and depth using many multi-dimensional methods. I pump up my words by employing the six senses. Step by step I multi-layer a story to fill it with substance and meaning. I show a story, stay out of the picture, and use consistency to keep the reader in the fictive dream. I keep readers suspended by strings rather than rope so that they are free to draw conclusions. My characters seem so real they can reach out and touch readers' hands.

~ Insight 64 ~

Where's the Draft Coming From?

Every draft I edit helps to perfect my manuscript and make it more professional. Drafts draw me nearer to successful publication because they're necessary to create a high quality piece. I'm in the writing game if I've given my manuscript all the drafts it needs to shine. I'm doing myself and readers a disservice if I shirk the drafts process.

It may feel tedious at times to comb through pages and straighten out all the knots in plots, sentence structures, inconsistencies, typos, and layout, but it must be done. Therefore, I take the task on full heartedly and plough through however many drafts my work requires to make it the best I can. It's exciting to watch my work shape up draft by draft, becoming a lean, clean machine that smoothly transports the reader to another place.

Drafts belong to the editing stage, but each one is a different level of improvement. It's like draft by draft I'm refining a painting by adding the intricate touches and defining strokes, by blending colours and shades, and by perfecting the depth, texture, consistency, and tone.

I value the effect that numerous drafts have on my end product so I move through them with confidence and determination. My first draft is always my boggiest. The middle ones are murky. My last draft needs to be as fluid and as clear as a mountain spring.

Sometimes it's difficult to judge whether my final draft needs more filtering because I've been immersed in the project for so long. Therefore, I come up for air and let the final draft sit for a while. When I read it again I can spot the impurities. Then I do the real final draft.

I use my intuition to tell me when to stop the drafts, knowing that they could continue forever if I let them and that the story would keep evolving over a lengthy period.

All works are individual. They each require a different number of drafts to reach the final one. On the fourth draft, the manuscript could be starting to take on its end form. Anywhere from six drafts onwards is usually where the gold lies. An author of a finished three hundred page book has probably edited at least 1,800 pages to get there.

Affirmation

I do what it takes to get the final draft done without griping or cutting corners. I keep my focus strong by keeping my eyes on the prize, being a shining manuscript. The blood, sweat, and tears I put into drafts build healthy flesh on my book's bones and breathe real life into it, helping to create a genuine contender in the marketplace.

~ Insight 65 ~

The Business of Business

I take time to look into the business of writing if I want to become a professional writer who earns a living from the craft. I may prefer to contemplate characters and their calamities, but I must have an understanding of how the writing industry works to increase my chances of succeeding in it. Ignorance in business is lazy, costly, causes pain, and wastes time.

I need to familiarise myself with how a professional writer operates so I can have a general idea of what to expect, what I may need to do at different stages, and how to respond when my work takes off in the marketplace and I earn an income.

A professional writer must be able to keep a stream of works flowing through the pipeline to promote and keep his or her name out there. I also need to interact well with other people such as editors, collaborators, legal representatives, illustrators, partners, or the public.

I learn how to format business correspondence in addition to title pages, emails, and manuscripts. I learn about pitching a book, writing kick-ass query and cover letters, preparing powerful proposals, and creating a One Sheet story rundown for one-on-one presentations.

I prepare a manuscript submission aiming to reduce the receiving editor's workload. For example, in my proposal I can provide research about my book's saleability by way of market comparisons. I can identify my book's point of difference and specify the precise target readership.

I become familiar with traditional and online publishing terms and conditions, charges and royalty rates, distribution, and rights. I learn about publishing contracts and find out which amendments and adjustments I could suggest that a publisher would accept. I identify the stipulations that I could ask a publisher to remove from the contract.

I learn the extent to which I should sell my rights and which ones I should keep or add. I research websites about intellectual property - for example at www.ipaustralia.gov.au or www.copyright.gov - to gain an understanding or overview of domestic and international copyright laws.

To commence and grow a business, I need to have a good understanding of how it best functions and what to expect in order to make informed decisions.

Affirmation

I may prefer writing's creative side, but I embrace the commercial aspect too. It serves me well to implement business sense as a professional writer if I hope to base my financial future on writing.

It's best I have a basic understanding of how commercial dealings work to be informed and prepared. This helps to lessen the surprises and increase my control.

I learn about the standard payment figures and contractual arrangements. I familiarise myself with common legal terms and intellectual property law.

I'd research the business side of any commercial endeavour before proceeding with it, so naturally I apply this approach to my writing business.

~ Insight 66 ~

Plagiarism Beats Obscurity

I expose my work to the world in the faith that editors and other writers have integrity. With trust I send my work into the public domain to see what sticks and what gets responses. I need my writing to find its way to the target readership.

My focus is on breaking through obscurity rather than guarding against plagiarism. I'd rather risk being read than remain invisible. Therefore, I send out my work without fear of being ripped off or copied. I want the world to read my writing in whichever way possible so that the attention may help my work take off in the marketplace.

If someone steals my manuscript, submits it to a publisher, and receives an acceptance, fantastic. Any success is likely to be noticed. So thanks for finding me the publisher. Now I'll claim what's rightfully mine in accordance with copyright and intellectual property laws.

If anyone copies my words and reaps rewards for my efforts, I can consider it a compliment and seek recompense by providing comparisons of my works and following the legal process. I can notify the industry and public online of any plagiarism acts against me.

Dated computer records, emails sent, the drafts in attachments that I've emailed to myself, hand written notes, plot trees and so on all serve as evidence that the original work is mine.

I can worry about plagiarism when I'm in demand. Right now I need to move past obscurity and have people want my work. I can use my website/blog and online publishing platforms to launch my writing into the world. I can give away some writing pieces to attract readership attention. I could write for free to gain exposure. I could participate in writers' festivals to help me become known. I could talk about my book at schools and libraries. I could give public readings. I just want my writing to be out there and working.

Affirmation

My main public concern is to break through obscurity. Therefore, I make contacts, present my writing, and publish my work without fear of plagiarism. I trust that the industry has integrity. I send my work into the public domain with faith. Besides, there are many ways to prove that I'm the original author of my work. I'm unconcerned about plagiarism. It's obscurity that has my attention.

~ Insight 67 ~

Be a Dream Catcher

As a writer it's my job to daydream on a regular basis. As part of my work ethic I make it a habit to let my mind roam without a leash. I take steps to untie my imagination from the tethers of ingrained concepts and contemplate ideas outside the square.

With Edward de Bono's lateral thinking approach in mind I consider solutions from horizontal, diagonal, vertical, back to front, and upside down viewpoints. I allow my mind to lie back and rest on absurd ideas. I jot down sleep dreams that are vivid and intriguing.

Wisps of promising visions and bizarre ideas float around me all the time. Fantasies can flutter past and whisper in my ears. Crazy notions can fly through my mind. Glimpses of *what if?s* can flash and disappear. Subconscious suggestions may come and go.

I need to become aware of these freewheeling, frivolous thoughts when they appear and summon them to settle upon me. I have the ability to grab their ethereal feathers and tie them into strong wings of imaginings that could lift my writing off the ground, help me forge new flight paths, and carry me towards my writing dreams.

Affirmation

I believe that ideas are infinite and everywhere. During my carefree, unbridled thought times I encourage uncommon notions to swoop in and settle upon me. I give my imagination the freedom to wander around and notice ideas from all directions. I invite visions to present themselves out of thin air without censorship or conditions.

I catch hold of fantastic feathery thoughts and tie them together into growing concepts that could turn into fully fledged projects ready to fly. Daydreaming gives my writing wings because, being a writer, I'm also a professional dream catcher.

~ Insight 68 ~

Be a Thought Watcher

It's easy to let my thoughts roll around, but it's easier on my writing career if I pull them apart and study them. I become conscious of my thought patterns to isolate their behaviour and note their effects on me.

Apparently ninety percent of a person's thoughts are the same each day. I make it a habit to observe my thoughts in order to ascertain whether they're counterproductive to my self-esteem and writing goals. I check my thoughts for repetitive, negative cycles and make a conscious effort to break them if they occur.

I take note of amusing thoughts to capture and retain puns, witty statements, ironies, and anecdotes. I look for connections between strings of thoughts that seem non-related. I study my thoughts to better understand my reasoning, responses, and perspective on life.

I retain mental notes on my surroundings to sharpen the specifics in my writing. I lock in people's reactions and the chains of events to which they belonged. Writers are in the business of watching their thoughts and speculating upon others', connecting thoughts in interesting ways, and moulding them into text that conveys meaning.

Affirmation

I develop the habit of stopping to observe my thoughts. I work on shielding my mind from thoughts that hinder my writing journey or serve no purpose. I meditate to help clear away negative thought patterns and encourage thinking that supports me and my dreams.

I use the power of thought observation in my writing. I become conscious of my perceptions and contemplate what others' might be based on their responses. I retain mental notes of meaningful connections, interesting occurrences, causes and reactions, and sharpened surroundings. In doing so, I become a more prolific writer.

~ Insight 69 ~

First Impressions – the Basics

When readers or editors glimpse the first few pages of a book they form a fast and firm first impression. Therefore, I take care that:

- My presentation is as professional as possible, adhering to standard industry layout requirements,
- I tend to use one single, most effective adjective at a time. I search for the best adjective that can substitute for two or more,
- I use a minimal amount of adverbs, if any,
- My work has a pleasant rhythm when I read it as well as being technically correct,
- I have only used analogy, similes, and metaphors to cut out long description that slows the prose down and to help me better convey an idea or image,
- I have avoided using bad or clichéd comparisons,
- My writing style is not too old-style, too flowery, too academic, too unnatural, too melodramatic, or inappropriate for the piece,
- I ensure that my very first sentence is simply about the story as opposed to trying to impress,
- I keep the subject who is doing the action clear so that the reader knows exactly who's doing what at all times.

The first few pages make or break expectations and determine whether the reader will put the book down or settle into it and read on.

Affirmation

To get to first base with a reader I ensure that the first few pages serve as a positive indication of the writing standard to follow. I employ several fundamental writing principles to pull the reader through the first pages and entice the reader to venture beyond. My writing strikes a pleasing chord from the outset and instils a sense of trust that the rest of the book is worth reading.

~ Insight 70 ~

Fear Less

Fear of failure and fear of success are both mindsets that drive away my writing dreams so I disregard them. Instead, I feel assurance in every written attempt I make because the ability to keep trying is the truest measure of accomplishment.

Persistence demonstrates my winning character and inner strength during my writing journey. It's misleading to base my success purely on publication offers, online sales, financial rewards, and/or public acclaim.

Fear of failure

The only way I can achieve writing success is by trial and error. A successful writer is never successful all the time, but attains victories by persevering through many defeats. Therefore, I'm fine with experiencing failure because this is the pathway to success. Also, persisting through failed attempts is a huge success in itself.

Fear of success

I'm successful when I finish writing a book and when I write regularly and when I complete a plot tree, submission, or layout, and when I refuse to let a rejection letter psyche me out. All these triumphs prove that I experience writing success often and that therefore I'm unafraid of success. The reality is that I handle writing accomplishments just fine.

What I need to fear is the failure to try since this would bring me deep remorse. I would regret wondering what could have been. Persistent attempts against adversity are the truest measure of success.

Affirmation

The only fear I have is of failing to try. I use perseverance as the yardstick to measure my writing success. The obstacles I overcome mark my true accomplishments. I refuse to live a life of regret and so keep on writing, taking note of all successes great and small that I experience and enjoy along the way.

~ Insight 71 ~

Make More Senses

As mentioned, it makes sense to employ all five physical senses in my writing. This helps me to show rather than tell a story. I add dimension and intimacy to the reader's experience this way. I add reality. After all, we have sensations beyond sight and sound and so do my protagonists. Non-fiction subjects can better relay their real life experiences too using the range of physical perceptions.

I observe my own physical experiences so I can employ the various sensations in my story and draw upon my sixth sense to provide me with a gut feeling to guide my writing choices. However, there's more. I use many other types of sense to enhance my writing.

I write with a sense of purpose. I sense what's important to write about. I use common sense when choosing a writing project to take on. I use rational sense to gauge whether the idea is a golden goer. I sense what the market might be lacking by researching what's available. I may offer my writing online for cents so that my work can compete and many readers can access it.

I use sense and sensibility to produce work that's satisfying. I use words to convey the sense of meaning I intend. I sense what my characters would do in specific circumstances based on their constitution. Readers sense what could happen next in the piece.

I remove nonsense from my plot sequences. I sense the writing I'm in love with and get rid of it. I sense ambiguity in my sentences and straighten them out. I sense more concise ways to say something and iron out grammatical wrinkles. I use my sense of humour to make my writing more appealing and to help carry me along the writer's journey.

Writing is an artistic, intuitive, sensual craft that requires much sense to arrive at a marketable draft.

Affirmation

I write using more than the five physical senses and intuitive sixth sense. I use sense in all senses of the word to create an appealing, publishable piece of writing. I edit in the strictest sense to help bring extreme sense to my words. Writing brings me to my senses in many valuable ways. I write to help make sense of the human condition and the world in which we live.

~ Insight 72 ~

Write to the Tune

The 'sound' of my writing comes from the basic sentence structure and the rhythm of its flow when I read it.

The 'style' of my writing relates to the sentence structure too, but in the way it communicates to the reader, such as in an archaic, technical, melodramatic, conversational, business, or literary style. I need to select the style that best suits the purpose of my writing.

I avoid writing in a convoluted, wordy, or exaggerated style so I may convey the message to the reader in a direct, clear manner. Words are the trees and the story is the forest. I want the reader to see the forest without the trees obstructing the view. This helps to ensure a strong, successful communication to the reader.

The 'tone' of my writing comes from the attitude in which I wrote the piece rather than from the sentence structure. Examples of tone include witty, sarcastic, serious, flippant, intimate, or distant. The tone of my writing is subjective and therefore is always right.

Affirmation

'Sound', 'style', and 'tone' are instruments that play together in my writing to orchestrate its tune and help produce my unique voice. I write my pieces and re-read them aloud. I do this to listen to the aural effects and to sense the emotive forces that my sound, style, and tone have created. I modify these instruments to help me produce the tune I want the reader to hear.

~ Insight 73 ~

Be Adjustable

If my current life challenges are demanding a lot from me I can adapt by undertaking short sharp writing projects that are easier to get my head around and finish. Or I can reduce the daily word or page edit count to a manageable amount.

If serious situations crop up that I must deal with I'm flexible about my writing times. I let go of any frustration and identify where else I could weave writing into my day. I live a life that involves other people, which is a good thing. So I accept that there'll be times when I may need to swap around my writing plans to take proper care of family, friends, and any pressing situations.

I may need to fix my writing times on a permanent flexible plan for a while. If this is the case, I avoid waiting for the perfect writing time to present itself. I become quick on the uptake and recognise the opportune moments as they arise. If a sudden small window of writing time appears I run over, open it, look out, and write. Practising this response helps break down any hesitation to write.

If writing time arrives, but I feel too fried or scrambled to centre myself I remain pliable and write anyway. I can write whatever I want if I'm unable to concentrate on what I'd planned to do. I can write about feeling exasperated and unsettled. I can write about holding onto my writing dreams regardless of how I may be feeling or how impossible my day has become. Calmer times will arrive sooner or later.

My mindset must be malleable when my life demands it to be in order for me to keep writing. As things change and I get more time to myself I'll be able to expand the scope of my writing assignments and take on more intensive projects on a routine basis. Times will come when I'll be able to better structure my writing periods and have less interruption. But until then I remain adjustable.

Affirmation

I can write every day, even if it's only for five minutes. I can reach my daily word count if it's only fifty words. I'm sensible in choosing appropriate writing projects and goals that suit my current life commitments.

I avoid being rigid with writing time slots. The day can often pan out differently to the way I expected. When this happens I shrug off frustration and move with the times. I work with the flow, being time resourceful. Whenever I spot opportune moments to write I seize them.

~ Insight 74 ~

Set Off the Fireworks

Readers want to know about my deep emotional experiences through the guise of my characters. They want to know the dread, the embarrassment, the love, the triumph, and the sorrow so they can compare their own experiences or access experiences outside of them. Therefore, I give readers the truth and give the big scenes in my story the utmost care so they may deliver an explosive experience.

For the climactic scenes I confront my deepest emotions and draw upon them. I avoid shying away from or skimping on the drama that readers expect the big scenes to have. I convey the most dramatic parts by relaying in gritty detail the emotional impact that a situation has on the characters. I can do this by showing a string of specific actions and emotional responses within the characters' frameworks. I refrain from using any descriptive narrative that tells the scene instead of shows it.

I lower my expectations of the first several drafts since the peak scenes can be challenging and take extra time to get right. They require a higher degree of observation and skill in order to fully move the reader and keep the fictive dream going. Although big scenes demand a lot from me the fireworks they launch can be mind-blowing if I write them well.

Affirmation

I give extra time and attention to writing the dramatic peaks in my story. I show my characters' raw emotional responses by drawing upon my own experiences with honesty. My characters undergo the physical sensations and use the dialogue that strong emotions can cause. I hold back nothing and load the drama by handing over all the juicy details. Doing this helps to ensure that the reader feels what my characters are experiencing and that the scene satisfies.

I embrace writing the heightened scenes because I'm excited about them. I take deep breaths, open up my heart, and trust that I'm able to set off the fireworks in my work.

~ Insight 75 ~

My Creative Space

I have a writing area at home. No matter how small it is or where it's located I take care of my creative space with the same diligence as the rest of the house. I make it as conducive as possible to writing which includes minimising noise interference.

I keep my writing area dust free. Like an indoor plant, light and air need to permeate it which helps my thoughts and writing blossom.

I treat my special place well by keeping it tidy, by furbishing it with decent writing tools, by supplying it with extra lighting if necessary, and by making it feel warm and inviting. I keep my writing place uncluttered to reflect my mindset and my written work. Having room to write and lay out paperwork allows my energy to flow around without obstruction.

The attention I give my writing area indicates that I give my writing attention, however I refuse to let over-cleaning get in the way of writing.

I bless my creative space with a lit candle, a flower in a vase, a scented oil burner, a small fish tank, or a potted plant to show my awareness and appreciation of the connection between my nature and this area.

I can decorate my creative station with a few meaningful items from people in my life or places I've been. I can put some successful books in sight. I can stick affirmations, my empowering beliefs, or an article about a successful writer on the wall as a friendly reminder of what I aim to achieve.

Affirmation

I'm mentally, physically, and spiritually connected to my writing place. I decorate my creative haven with significant objects that help invoke inspiration, memories, and emotions such as feelings of safety and serenity. I make the space as comfortable as I can to help me feel enticed to use it. I respect my work station by keeping it clean without needing it to be spotless and sterile. I'm thankful for my writing place.

~ Insight 76 ~

Write In the Zone

I write best when I'm in the zone. Ironically, it's a comfortable zone where I write with little or no effort. I slip into what feels like an autonomous state where words pour out of me from some place other than my conscious mind. Time awareness vanishes. Any struggle to find something to say is gone. Turning thoughts into written words seems instantaneous and I feel like I'm riding the wind. When I land I'm amazed at how fast time flew. I'm surprised by what I read and how much I've written. A borderless aspect of me has been expressing itself, revealing its wisdom.

I love writing in the zone. It's so effortless and feels so right. I prepare by taking several long deep breaths to strengthen the connection between the physical and metaphysical realms since air is the bridge that connects the two. I become quiet and calm. I go to my sanctuary and feel safe.

I can meditate to empty my mind and prepare to receive. I can call upon the writers in spirit to be by my side and bless me with their vibrations. Often writing by hand is more effective than typing. Writing in the zone is the most pleasurable and spiritual way to write.

Affirmation

I prefer to write in the comfortable zone. I give myself permission to be free and write whatever comes. I renew faith in my ability. I trust in my higher self and my intuition. I ask my creative right brain to step forwards and take the lead ahead of the rational, judgemental left brain.

I take deep breaths. I slip into the blissful autonomous state and write. My thoughts flow out of me without reserve. Later I'll use my rational mind to edit and mould what I get down into a form fit for reading. I love riding the wind of unbridled creativity on the steed of my subconsciousness.

~ Insight 77 ~

Invite Master Lady Nada

I invite Lady Nada to visit me. I ask the Ascended Master to remove any false material or misinformation from my words as I write. I ask Lady Nada to bless my work with her truth vibration and help me convey the human condition and the world with correctness.

I bid Lady Nada to give me the tools and experiences I require to improve my writing. I ask for her assistance to render my work acceptable and useful to others in order to fulfil their needs.

I ask the Ascended Master to help me see past ingrained beliefs and traditions so I may view the world with fresh eyes and convey it through new perspectives. May Lady Nada remove judgement from my writing so that my work is fair and untwisted, granting readers the freedom to form their own opinions.

I ask Lady Nada to help me ward off any tendency to be self-critical when I write so that my work is uninhibited and comes from a higher consciousness.

Affirmation

Lady Nada, please guide me to see what my writing requires in order for it to shine and fulfil readers' needs. Please present the knowledge and experiences that would help me progress on every level and achieve my dreams. Assist me to process and employ the knowledge I acquire so I may be an excellent, useful writer.

I request that you help me find time in which to write. Please help me find balance so I may function better and contribute more. Please help me understand others' needs so that I may serve them well. Above all, please bestow upon humankind whatever it needs, rather than wants, in order to evolve and find peace.

~ Insight 78 ~

Humility

I'm humble enough to submit my work for free to gain writing credits and exposure. I'm detached enough from my writing to give it away to help develop a readership. It's okay to start at the start and even go back to the start. I value any public attention my writing receives even if it's unpaid because this is a means to an end.

Whatever keeps me writing is good. Whatever builds my writing reputation is great. I get excited whenever I see my work in print or online. Any publication renews my vow to keep writing.

I may trigger someone's interest from a free article I've written. Winning a writing competition would help build up my Curriculum Vitae. I might spark someone's imagination from a free story I published online or contributed to a publication. All these possibilities may lead to collaboration on a writing project, a permanent writing position, requests for more of my work, and followers. In addition, I'm creating material to blog about and put on my website.

There are many signs that can indicate I'm faring well along my writing journey: winning a prize, receiving positive posts and reviews for the writing I've given away, gaining followers who share my writing interests, receiving a compliment from a novel assessment company, and attracting visitors to my website or blog.

Publishing credits, awards, and positive feedback for any types of writing reflect my success. However, the most important marker is my unwavering resolve to keep writing.

Affirmation

I accept that writing and submitting for free maybe what I need to do to enter or re-enter the industry. I may need to write without financial reward in order to help promote the work I already have for sale. I may need to use my writing to get my foot in the door and network for me.

I make my writing available to the public so it may lead to solicited work and create a readership following. Giving away my writing is a temporary measure that's a diligent, calculated step towards living the professional writer's life.

~ Insight 79 ~

Give and Receive

Giving and receiving is a basic universal law of balance, fairness, and order. When I give a reader my best writing I receive joy in creating, completing, and attaining excellence. I might also gain acknowledgement, support, and/or financial reward. I could receive a serendipitous opportunity.

I receive joy in giving when I give full heartedly. Sometimes I may give without realising and remain unaware of the positive impact I've had on a person or situation. Either way I receive kind reciprocation from the universe. I receive blessings from different sources at various times, some of which may appear unrelated to my giving act, but they are.

If I give time and effort to creating a great reading experience the reader might give time to reading my work. If I give heartfelt honesty to readers they might give me their hearts. If I give my work away to help others I might receive demand for my writing along with other rewards.

I give from a good place. I give to participate in life's natural, positive flow of exchange. Otherwise my intentions could be hollow and manipulative, making what I receive unpleasant. I write my best for the reader and give with integrity.

Affirmation

I give myself willingly to the service of writing for others. With integrity I give to readers to establish a mutually beneficial relationship. Although I'm unsure what I'll receive in return for my efforts, I already get joy from writing and from owning my dreams.

I give my writing all I've got in the faith that the universe is fair, kind, and can work wonders in unexpected ways. I write from a good place that attracts good in return. I'm part of life's positive exchange.

~ Insight 80 ~

Step into the Pro's Life Daily

Every day I make the professional writer's life mine by taking action that belongs to it. I shift my focus from the life I'm living and put it on the life I want to live. I behave like a fulltime writer as much as possible in order to become one, which includes shunning procrastination and writing without waiting for inspiration to hit me.

A professional writer writes to earn a living. If I envision that a fulltime writer starts the day writing I get up earlier to enable me to do so too. I work out ways to write during the day. I write at night to make a deadline just as a professional writer would. My goal is to build up to writing two thousand words a day.

I think about viable projects, plots, and angles as if writing is already my business. I factor in time frames and abide by completion dates. I have my writer's station and tools. I write as efficiently as I can. I tell people I'm a writer if they ask what I do.

I communicate with other writers and industry professionals. I send out submissions and proposals regularly. I'm part of the writing network through emails, enquiries, writing festivals, and groups. I accept criticism and am willing to co-operate with professionals to get my work right.

I learn about the business side of writing and consider my projects as products. I finish what I start and whip my work into shape until it's fit for public consumption. I have several writing projects going on at once which helps to keep me keen and busy, just like a professional writer.

I explore diverse avenues for earning income such as writing e-books, magazine articles, columns, greeting cards, blogs, copy writing and more. I'm open to making money from a variety of sources at the same time. Most fulltime writers write every day in several areas to earn a decent, consistent living.

Affirmation

I step into the fulltime writer's life as much as possible. I wear the professional writer's shoes and behave as an experienced writer would on a daily basis even if it's for a short period of time. I aim to build my daily word count up to two thousand.

I'm thick-skinned towards rejections and criticism as is the seasoned writer. I'm open to making improvements to my work based on industry advice.

I expect my writing to earn income from various sources. I avoid procrastination at all costs and write when it's inconvenient. I start writing before inspiration arrives. Every day my actions assert the reality that I'm a career writer who means business.

~ Insight 81 ~

Be an Attitude Athlete

Apparently ninety percent of people dream about writing a book. Five percent of them make the attempt. However, I'm in the top one percent of writers who finish their books because I maintain momentum on a healthy attitude. I'm dedicated to the dream and work towards it with faith, hope, and planning. My attitude is an elite athlete that combats defeat and sneers at setbacks. It bounces back and rises to any challenge.

Movement creates movement. I exercise consistent action which helps to motivate me and keep my positive attitude strong. I want the dreams so much that my thoughts talk the talk and I walk the walk. I stick to my daily writing target exercise and often shoot past it. I complete marathon writing projects using determination and method.

A well-trained attitude is a major factor in my success. My attitude must flex its pecs against bouts of low or staggered writing activity. It must muscle up against jabs from negative thoughts. I have what it takes to reach my writing dreams because my attitude has the brawn to carry me there.

Affirmation

I'm passionate about my craft and goals. My attitude knocks negativity on the head. I always finish the projects I start and I maintain momentum by attending to my dreams on a regular basis. I'm filled with enthusiasm because I see my projects materialising and my dreams coming closer day by day. I'm meant for writing success and I have the elite mind-set I require to achieve it. I'm an attitude athlete.

~ Insight 82 ~

Works in Progress

Just like my current writing projects, I'm a work in progress, a fluid creation. I may consist of about sixty percent water, but I'm fluid in many other ways. Every day I respond to my environment, food, sleep, relationships, circumstances, desires, fears and more.

My thoughts can float, sink, rise, and whirlpool. My outlook can expand and contract. My emotions may come in waves that create ripple effects on others' lives and my surroundings.

What I physically and mentally pour into my body can alter its state. My skin cells flow through a complete regenerative process every seven days, my skeletal cells every seven years.

My belief system can solidify or melt. My aura's energy can swell. My spirit can be calm in the eye of a storm and my spirituality can wash away fears. My spiritual advancement can change the course of my life.

Thinking and acting in a way that opposes my dreams or my desire for positive change is aiding undesirable creation. It replaces my cells, and therefore my existence, using a counterproductive driving force.

I'm able to change things about myself daily. I can substitute or tweak them. I can sort out clutter, convolution, and contradiction in my life. I can mould myself step by step into what I envision.

Even the smallest actions impact on me and play a part in shaping my existence. This can be difficult to feel or see at the time. Their immediate impact may be undetectable, but over time they can compound to create significant effects.

Affirmation

I'm a fluid work in progress physically, mentally, emotionally, and spiritually. I'm unable to remain stagnant contrary to how I may be feeling sometimes.

I'm mindful that every small action I take matters and can create change for the better. Every little decision I make partakes in cause and effect. The generative cells in my body and words in my manuscript take part in cause and effect.

Every day I do what I can to work on the project called *Me*. I regenerate my attitude and renew my dreams. I apply the same positive creative force to myself as I do to my writing projects.

Minute by minute I can shape myself into the person I want to be and my life into the one I envision. I value present moments, knowing they have an important accumulative effect on my future.

~ Insight 83 ~

Entitled

A title is entitled to my full attention. A title represents a body of writing and provides the first impression to the reader, making it a vital marketing tool. Titles have an important job to do so I give them as much time as I need to get them right.

If 'non-writers' knew how much time writers tend to spend on titles they'd think we were mad. It does seem crazy to give so much time to so few words, but the title must work. It must catch readers' attention and stick in their minds.

To turn heads a title needs to create interest and intrigue, evoke an image and an emotional response, be concise and perhaps witty, and have relevant meaning that makes fair sense to the reader of what's to come. Titles are like ideas in the way that they're generally unable to be copyrighted, but the best titles are those that are unlike any of the ones that have been used.

Titles with an odd number of words or that consist of three to five syllables sound sharper. Words that begin with strong sounding letters can be effective too.

I brainstorm and let title ideas sit on my mind for a while. The best time to work on my title is when I've finished the manuscript because that's the point when I know my product best and can pinpoint what it's truly about.

Affirmation

I choose a title when I complete my manuscript so that I can identify the bottom line and capture the end product well. I consider various titles for a considerable time before choosing the best one because titles are important marketing tools. I make a long list of options and never rush to employ the first titles that come to mind.

I ruminate on titles. I let them sit on my palette to savour their sound, rhythm, sauciness, and meaning. I say them aloud to hear their aural impact. I look for titles that have the x-factor in them and avoid using ones that sound self-important or vague so that I entice the reader to read my work.

~ Insight 84 ~

I Am a Co-Creator

I co-create on many levels. I co-create with the world in every aspect of my life.

My thoughts and actions co-create with the environment and with other people to help shape our surroundings and lives. My thoughts and speech co-create my voice in response to the world and this can influence others. My writing co-creates experiences, outlooks, concepts, and worlds with a reader's mind.

The internal and external words that I use, along with my actions, have a direct impact on the results of my co-creation. Therefore, I keep buffing my words with enthusiasm and open-mindedness to help prevent them from becoming dusty, dull, or destructive. I polish my written words so that they may sparkle and co-create prisms of light with the mind of the person who reads them.

Affirmation

I'm always co-creating. When my thoughts, words, and actions co-create in a positive way I help manifest a positive reality with other people and the environment. I can help produce occurrences capable of bringing blessings to me and others. It's always a privilege for my writing to co-create worlds, thoughts, emotions, and experiences with a trusting reader.

~ Insight 85 ~

Tough Love

I give my writing tough love to draw out the best in it. This helps my writing to stand tall on its own out in the world. Tough love is tough to deliver; it requires discipline and detachment.

There are many ways in which I treat my writing with tough love. For example, I refuse wayward words. I demand that sentences be clear and specific. I oust passive phrases that lie around like sloths, wasting the reader's time and zapping strength from my communication.

I remove any parts of my writing that I'm in love with because romantic love is blind and indulgent. I remove frilly words that flirt and try to have their way with me. I ignore my ego and eliminate proud writing from my prose otherwise the text is at risk of being convoluted, distant, and ambiguous. Every word must perform its duty and contribute to the overall piece.

I give my writing real love - honest love - that pulls my words into line and makes them behave properly in order to produce the best communicative results. I give my writing boundaries to help it survive and succeed in the real world. Tough love is like a stake in the ground that supports my writing and guides it upwards.

Affirmation

I'm strict with my writing because I care about it. I ensure my work is well-groomed and disciplined in order to give it the best chance to succeed in the public domain. I refuse to let leniency and laziness harm my writing. I bar delinquent words that try to lead it astray. I only let in hardworking words that convey my messages in the strongest, clearest, and most concise way.

~ Insight 86 ~

Forgive and Forgiven

I forgive myself for the periods in my life when I neglected to write. There were times when I pushed my writing dreams away and withdrew my resolve. There were times when I had less courage and conviction to write than what I have today.

I forgive myself for failing to put on my writer's hiking boots and follow my compass at the outset. At times I dragged my feet along the way and allowed the sideline scenery to side-track me. Sometimes I miscalculated the sun's position.

I forgive myself for the times I believed in other people's strengths more than my own and allowed myself to follow them instead of my dreams. I forgive myself for granting others the power to make my decisions when I felt vulnerable and confused.

I forgive those people who discouraged my writing dreams because they believed it was best for me. I forgive them for being unsupportive due to their own insecurities and fears.

I forgive myself for failing to realise sooner what writing meant to my higher self and that I needed to write in order to have a happier soul.

Times past are irreversible, so I put them behind me and make the most of the time I have from here on. I stand firm on the path and march straight forwards wasting no more time on my writer's journey.

Affirmation

Today I'm different. I know that writing is mine and I refuse to let it go. I give writing my time, love, and attention, keeping my eyes open for opportunities. I've learned many lessons from pursuing winding roads instead of following a straight route to my dreams so there's no regret, just resolve to stay on track. Besides, the winding roads have given me lots to write about.

~ Insight 87 ~

Consistency is King

Career book authors use consistency for more than creating solid, stunning manuscripts with reliable characters, steady plots, and uniform story details. They use consistency to achieve more than their daily word or page edit count. Successful book authors need to consistently write appealing, professional books to keep up sales in order to derive a financially sustainable living from them.

Becoming a published book author can seem like the most important destination, but it's only first base. Book authors need to try as hard, if not harder, on subsequent book projects to produce a steady flow of lucrative publications.

A traditional publisher or the target readership may reject a popular debut author's second book. The publisher and readers' expectations may be riding high from the first and this pressure could make it harder for the author to write the next successful manuscript. Therefore, the first publication is far from the be all and end all. Rather, it's the start of a stage in the writer's journey. As a book author, my long term goal then is to consistently create books that people want to read.

Affirmation

It's unlikely that my first publication will set me up for life. A long journey lies beyond my first financially rewarding book. Therefore, I avoid getting hung up on the manuscript I'm working on. I extend the vision of my book author career way beyond my first success to include a string of popular, lucrative publications.

I write every book well and get it out there as soon as possible because I have many books yet to write. I apply just as much, if not more, passion and diligence to the subsequent books I write in order to exceed expectations. My consistency in producing marketable manuscripts is a king component of my book author success.

~ Insight 88 ~

Learn From Successful Writers

Career writers encourage me. They affirm that professional writing success is achievable in a myriad of ways. They strengthen my belief that writing can be a viable way to earn a living. Successful writers help intensify my ambition.

I admire how seasoned writers are skilled at fulfilling readers' needs and writing sellable material. I applaud the professional writer's ability to create work and present it well to the world, having used their intuitive powers and common sense to gauge what to write about.

I respect every professional writer's journey to success even if it seems like it happened overnight or appears too good to be true. I use any success story to inspire me, stir me to action, and strengthen my resolve.

Multi-published, well-paid authors are especially marvellous. The high earning, publicly acclaimed novelists are an extra special breed. I acknowledge their chronic hard work on intricate, lengthy manuscripts and their ability to deliver outstanding stories time and time again. I applaud their mental resilience, the widths-heights-depths of their imaginations, the tenacity to return with more in store, their survival techniques, their adaptability, their self-promotion, and their unconditional love for writing.

Affirmation

I respect all types of financially sustainable writers and applaud their achievements. I learn from their examples and leadership rather than envy them or feel inferior. Their strength, creativity, skill, and dedication inspire me. I like to find out what makes them tick. I consider why the public loves a particular writer's works so I may better understand the prerequisites for market success.

Multi-published authors sit alone at their desks and ponder about what to write like I do. They have just done so more often and keep hitting the target with appealing stories and professional writing. So I learn from them. I keep aiming and writing too.

~ Insight 89 ~

The Magic Never Leaves

In the past my writing has shone and I've received acknowledgement for it. People have told me I had writing talent and I trusted them. I wrote naturally and freely without apprehension or pressure. The child in me wrote with faith and unbridled enthusiasm. My imagination was so supple that whole stories flowed out onto the page in one sitting. Writing was my special gift and it rewarded me.

Sometimes I wonder if my writing still reflects that same strong light. Do I still have the same magic people told me I possessed? Do I have enough magic to compete, make a name for myself, and become a career writer?

The answer is yes. There are many talented and devoted writers who experience less writing success than they expected although the magic resides within them. Faith and perseverance are the qualities that separate the winning writers from the wannabes.

My internal dialogue must stay afloat during shipwreck writing periods. All writers encounter shadowy waves of self-doubt. We all get hit by swells of disappointment. The rips of despondency can drag each one of us down. We all fail to reach personal expectations at times and can feel like sardines in a murky ocean.

The writers who refuse to drown are the ones who know in their hearts that the writing magic never leaves them and with practice it gets stronger. At times the magic may seem to disappear, but the truth is it's always there.

Affirmation

I'm a fighter-writer fish who swims against adverse currents. I tackle days of defeat. I elude the nets that try to trap me into quitting. I escape the negative self-talk that attempts to hook me into believing that I've lost what it takes to shine. I'll always possess the writer's magic. And upon that awareness I swim forwards on my writing journey, employing all fins.

~ Insight 90 ~

Advocate

Being a writer, my penchant for correct spelling, grammar, and punctuation can irritate 'non-writers'. However, my compulsion to maintain the integrity of textual language is my inbuilt defence mechanism against poor writing and is fundamental to my writing success. Proper writing allows me to create publishable pieces of work.

The writing rules help to maintain the language's shape and functionality. If a writer presents a piece full of grammatical mistakes, it's like displaying a streaky, cracked mirror in a shopfront or singing on stage with a croaky voice. The outcome is failure to deliver the goods.

Out of love and respect for the written word I tend to draw people's attention to grammar and spelling mistakes. I humbly share my knowledge of the rules to protect the language, uphold standards, and help others learn.

I'm open to variations of spelling from around the world. I'm interested in how language grows and evolves over time. I keep up with commonly accepted grammatical and spelling changes. I'm aware of new words that become part of communication and enter the modern dictionary. However, I remain opposed to careless writing.

Affirmation

I love the written language and help to uphold its integrity in society. I support literacy in a considerate, compassionate way. I'm open to modernised ways of writing and new commonly accepted rules. I'm obsessive when I check my work for grammar, punctuation, and spelling errors. The quality of my writing depends on it.

~ Insight 91 ~

Introvert

These days it seems I need to be an extrovert to become a successful writer. It's apparent that I need to put myself out there and promote my work although writing tends to be a reclusive craft that relies on the introvert in me to shine. I take this paradox as a challenge to develop a different aspect of me rather than as a conflict of character.

I may tend to feel more comfortable writing than speaking, but there are occasions when I do behave in an extroverted manner. Therefore, socialising physically and virtually to promote myself and my work will strengthen a less developed part of me, helping me to become well-rounded.

Taking steps to overcome shyness and self-consciousness helps to move myself forwards and improve my self-image. Becoming open to public interaction will broaden my life experiences and bring my writing dreams closer. It will encourage more writing opportunities. So I accept that I may need to be a socially confident person at times and know that I'll grow more accustomed to this as I go.

I'm open to self-promotion and marketing my work in the belief that my writing can serve to entertain, inform, and/or support its readers. Readers deserve to have access to the writers they take the time to read and I owe this to them.

It's common survey knowledge that people tend to fear public speaking more than death so I congratulate myself on being open to appearing in the public domain as a writer. Talking about my writing is simply an extension of my work.

I take baby steps if I have to. To start, I could make an enthusiastic internet video introducing myself as a writer with aspirations and talking about my work. Any online queries from readers and followers will require written responses, giving me time to think about how to reply, so this step is fine. One-on-one interviews, library appearances, and book signings may occur somewhat down the track, so most likely I'll have time to work my way up to this level of public interaction.

I prepare myself for public interaction by getting tips on public speaking and by observing how other writers step into the limelight. I learn how to project the socially confident side of me. It's okay to be a less than perfect extrovert. It's more important to enjoy the experiences and have integrity. I just need to be myself with enthusiasm and perhaps a little refinement. I accept the challenge because I'm worthy of taking my place in society as an interactive, accessible writer.

~ Insight 92 ~

Along the Writer's Journey

Along the way I share my writing knowledge and spirit with other writers. If the right situation presents itself I suggest constructive ways to strengthen another writer's creation and accept the same in return.

When possible I support the writers I meet by attending their promotional events, buying copies of their books, liking their websites, and contributing positive comments to their social media pages. We can learn and draw strength from each other.

The writer's journey can feel cold, lonely, dark, and barren at times and therefore I'm grateful for what other writers share with me along the way such as mutual understanding, a hot tip, an insight, information, a quip, a quote, a contact, a success story, and advice.

During the journey I can assist 'non-writers' and less experienced writers out of good will and with modesty. I appreciate everyone's efforts to write, despite whether they produce professional pieces, because all people are works in progress. Some people may struggle to spell the shopping list correctly or understand when to use capital letters or remember how to use apostrophes or get homonyms mixed up.

Some writers may be learning what I have known for a while, but I remain humble and respectful no matter how far along the road I've advanced. There will always be writers further ahead than me.

Affirmation

It can be difficult to go the writer's journey alone so I make my route a more pleasant experience by sharing my writing interests and knowledge with others along the way. I interact with writers in support of mutually beneficial professional relationships that help preserve the endurance and belief required to stay on the journey. I help others with writing where I can and receive many happy returns.

~ Insight 93 ~

First Impressions Count with Characters

To help rouse the reader's interest in my characters and maintain it I need to present my characters well from the outset by ensuring that:

- I keep the format of the names for my characters consistent, for example, I always use the first name, last name, full name, or nickname,
- I give my characters interesting names, avoiding highly exotic or annoyingly long names,
- I launch into the story while establishing some of the characters at the same time,
- I introduce my characters to the reader at a pace the reader can cope with,
- I have a very identifiable, dominant protagonist,
- I need every character in the story for it to work,

- I have specific, rather than generic characters,
- I have memorable characters,
- The reader will care about my characters and sympathise with the protagonist, even if the protagonist is hard to like.

Characters are the life of the story. It's imperative that they're lifelike, have purpose, and impact on the reader. However, it's upon the first meetings with them that the reader decides whether to stick around to witness their fates.

Basic fundamentals help the reader open up and let the characters in. Good first impressions encourage the reader to develop a deeper connection with the characters, giving them the opportunity to leave a long-lasting impression on the reader.

Affirmation

I take care to keep the character-reader relationship alive. The first step is to start their introduction by adhering to some basic protocols. I'm mindful that good first impressions are crucial in persuading the reader to grant permission for my characters to continue on and forge a deeper connection. I do my best to set up the first meetings in a way that will give my characters the opportunity to leave long-lasting impressions on the reader.

~ Insight 94 ~

Employ the Decoy

If I struggle with an aspect of a large project or start to feel as if the project will never end, I employ the decoy. I switch to a smaller project for a bit to free up my mind and refresh my perspective. My subconscious is then under no pressure from my rational conscious mind to deliver the answer I need to move forwards with the large project. This also helps to alleviate any frustration and despondency that could compound if I continued to be at loggerheads with the more complex project.

Smaller projects can be helping hands to bigger projects. Smaller projects can transform me into a rolling stone again rather than me remaining at a standstill and at risk of gathering moss. They can pull me out of the ditch.

When I pursue the smaller project decoy and finish it in a timely way I get a dose of accomplishment, which helps to fuel me with the positive energy I need to face the large project again. And by this time, my subconscious may be ready to supply me with the solution.

Affirmation

I know the value of having a few projects on the go at once. It's unnecessary for me to ever stop writing. It's okay if I hit a mental snag or run out of stamina with a project. I simply employ the easier decoy project and get that done as fast as possible. Then I go back to the more complex project with renewed verve and most likely with the solutions that my subconscious delivers.

~ Insight 95 ~

Boys and Girls Come Out to Play

I accept that I need regular play time in order to carry on with the business of writing. Play time allows me to rest, recuperate, and reset the mind frame I need to help me write. This is similar to how a mother can cope better with her children after she's enjoyed a little time out.

During leisure I relax and release tension. I daydream, laugh, and socialise. I give my intense writer's concentration a break. All work and no play can make me dull. However, I avoid using too much play time as a procrastination device against writing.

Rather than looking at play time as a waste of writing time I regard it as a necessary component to keep me writing long distance and to avoid burning out. Play time is a precaution against becoming a workaholic or hermit-like writer. It helps to preserve balance.

Also play time gives my subconscious mind room to flow around and form answers. Play time allows me to notice beauty, joy, and humour, which I can then transfer to my writing.

Play time could be an amble along the beach or through a park. I could watch a comedy with a friend or play a game with children. I could go out for dinner. I could snuggle up with someone I love.

Affirmation

I give myself enough play time to enable me to return to writing feeling replenished and ready for more. I embrace play time for what it provides - a break from the intensity of writing - and like sleep, I'm unable to function without it. Regular play time is necessary for me to enjoy a balanced life.

~ Insight 96 ~

Invite Master Sanat Kumara

Although thoughts are in essence intangible they are real and can quickly manifest physical, emotional, and spiritual effects. Thoughts can impact on me, my surroundings, and other life forms on different levels and in various dimensions. The documentary *I Am* demonstrated that Tom Shadyac's emotional state directly affected the energy level of yoghurt organisms nearby.

Thoughts can become spoken and written words, concepts displayed in material form, and actions taken. Therefore, I ask Master Sanat Kumara, whom people recognise as planetary logos of Earth, for help in channelling productive thoughts into my writing and speech that have a positive effect on me and the world.

May all people see themselves as light, as the Master does, and enjoy the beauty and colours of existence. May all people realise the extreme power of thoughts and exercise wisdom in thinking them.

Affirmation

I invite Master Sanat Kumara to bestow upon me positive energy from the highest source and deliver me from fruitless and destructive thoughts. I strive for consistency in thinking productive thoughts. I aim to lift my vibration and in turn influence others to lift theirs. I monitor my thoughts and refrain from applying negative ones to my writing, perceptions, visions of the future, and relationships.

I call upon Master Sanat Kumara to help remove negative thoughts from Earth. I ask him to raise the collective consciousness of humankind at a fast rate to expedite our evolution.

~ Insight 97 ~

Box of Tricks

If part of a writing project stumps me or I feel overwhelmed by the task at hand, I inhale deeply and relax. Besides employing the smaller project decoy, I have the option to reach into my box of tricks and pull out other methods to get me over the hurdle.

I can work on an easier aspect of the project to make some headway and lift my morale. For example, I could write the email that I'll send with my proposal, or flesh out a less complicated plot point, or get my characters' personal attributes down on cards for reference, or work on the title and cover. Putting the tougher part of the project aside gives my subconscious time to contemplate the obstacle and work on the answer.

I can break down the tricky part into bite sized pieces to digest the challenge instead of choking on chunks of it. Or I can dissect the whole project and give myself deadlines by which to complete smaller tasks, helping me to feel grounded. I can also swap the deadline of an obstinate challenge with an easier one. This way I relieve pressure, yet remain productive.

I can leave the area to temporarily change my environment and shake off heavy vibrations. I can meditate or envision my dreams fulfilled. I can contemplate the cover of my book, or visualise the manuscript as a movie, and so on. Such images fire me up to reapproach the tricky parts with a positive, passionate attitude, making me more susceptible to a breakthrough.

I can use the promise of reward to pull me through the discomfort I'm experiencing when grappling with an obstacle. For example, when I complete a small writing task - such as completing a fiddly paragraph to satisfaction - I can reward myself with a quick treat or pampering to acknowledge my efforts and mark the little victory.

I can reflect on what it is about the tricky part that concerns me. Knowledge is bliss; if I face the reason why the task is presenting as an obstacle and put this into perspective, the task tends to become less formidable. I understand myself better and can identify what may be triggering the block.

I can allocate only ten minutes to working on the tricky part. Reverse psychology tends to entice me to spend a lot longer than that on the challenge.

Or I can do a mundane chore to temporarily divert my intense scrutiny away from the stumbling block and free up my thoughts.

Affirmation

I have many methods up my sleeve to help me overcome the trickier parts of projects. Because of this I remain confident in the face of any writing block that may crop up.

I refuse to let negative emotions get in the way of moving through the challenges and finishing the project. I have the tools and power to adjust my mindset. I firmly believe that there's always a solution and that I'm meant to overcome the challenges that appear in my way.

~ Insight 98 ~

Intersperse Duties

Instead of performing all of my non-writing duties first up and in one long block I intersperse them with writing periods. This way I'm more likely to feel balanced and content throughout the day. I'm less likely to begrudge the chores and commitments that obstruct me from writing. I can write during lunch times and breaks if necessary.

If I complete all my chores first I may become too tired to handle one long writing session. I may be in a sterile frame of mind after cleaning all day. Undertaking a long block of repetitive, menial tasks can be heavy duty on the mind, dulling my creativity. It can also be physically exhausting and spiritually flattening. I may lose my appetite to write afterwards.

When I interchange duties and writing I feel like I'm making progress in both areas of my life. I can think about writing matters during stints of chores and then feel the satisfaction of getting those thoughts down in a timely manner. Chores give people time to contemplate and think matters through before taking action.

The reality is that the chore list never ends. By the time I get to the end of it the first chore needs to be done again. So I take this on board knowing that it's okay for chores to wait their turn while I write a bit.

Interspersing duties and writing also allows me to look after my body since lengthy writing periods can cause physical pain and discomfort. Writing for hours can be mentally exhausting so frequent breaks in the form of simple chores complements my writing program. Alternating helps to maintain productivity and a positive attitude all day long.

Affirmation

The best way to start the day is to work on my writing project, even if it's just for ten minutes. This helps to renew my higher purpose and reinforces the outlook that my dreams are top priority.

I interchange duties and writing throughout the day to help keep my spirits lifted and my energy level high. Interspersing tasks also serves to keep my body comfortable. When I pay regular attention to my higher self's needs I keep my soul balanced and happy.

~ **Insight 99** ~

All Writing Benefits Me

I use many types of writing in my life. Although some forms are for job or personal needs rather than for my dreams, I value all opportunities to write.

The general purpose writing that I use daily may not excite me or fan my imagination. The specialised writing I might do at work may feel dry, repetitive, and tedious. I might even feel that my writing skills are helping someone else achieve their dreams more often than mine.

What I have to write may feel like obstacles in the way of what I want to write. However, I can turn my attitude around and see the value in mundane writing chores.

General purpose and job related writing helps me move towards my dreams by forcing me to practise succinct writing and effective editing fast and frequently. It helps me get used to conveying direct messages with strength and clarity. Such tasks usually require minimal use of adverbs and adjectives and contain straightforward descriptions of events or ideas. They may also require professional formatting and help sharpen my eye for errors. All these skills help me improve my writing for both fiction and non-fiction projects.

Common or job specific writing tasks strengthen the wiring of my writer's brain. They train me to be adept at organising thoughts and forming them into a coherent presentation whether as a letter to the local council, a complaint to a company, a job application, a legal document, advertising copy, and so on. Helping out family and friends with written tasks also gives me practice in transferring others' thoughts into text with accuracy.

Affirmation

I recognise daily all-purpose writing tasks as opportunities to practise cutting out flowery language, to spot and remove passive phrases, to communicate as much as I can in the least words possible, to train my eye for presentation and correct punctuation, and to execute tasks in a timely manner.

Instead of letting life's mundane writing chores bore and bother me, I regard them as a means to improve my craft in pursuit of excellent and economical writing skills fit for a professional writing career.

~ Insight 100 ~

Hand It Over

If troubles plague me and the solutions remain elusive I hand the worries over to universal intelligence. I ask this supreme ordering force for its help, trusting that it will tend to my concerns with love and meticulous wisdom. It has the power to resolve matters in ways I'm unable to imagine.

I release the burden of solving deadlocked situations by opening a mental door and sending the problems out to infinite knowledge for a resolution. I could imagine packing a puzzle in a box and launching it into space in the faith that the universe will solve the puzzle in the best way possible.

I could use writing as a crowbar to help dislodge the worries from me and get them onto paper. I could then screw up the paper and bin it, having asked the universe to dispose the contents for me. This may be useful to do before working on a project since stress can distract focus, hinder clarity, and undermine confidence. It can obstruct my writing flow.

The universe is capable of working in mysterious ways on account of its omnipotence and omniscience. It presents endless miracles and overcomes seemingly impossible challenges. The world survives innumerable catastrophes and changes.

My troubles in comparison are small and easy. Solutions are on their way.

Affirmation

I keep my composure if a solution evades me or if the hope of healing a relationship is weak. A persistent problem is like a bullet under my skin so I ask the universe to work it to the surface and relieve me from its pain. In faith I hand over the impossible puzzles, thanking the cosmic force for applying its loving assistance and supreme wisdom to me.

References

20 Master Plots and How to Build Them by Ronald B. Tobias

2014 Digital Book World and Writer's Digest Author Survey

Children's Writing Super System by Christopher Maselli

Conclave Course by Mark Rolton

Daily Messages from Guardian Angels by Doreen Virtue

Hamlet, Act 2 Scene 2, lines 90-91 by Shakespeare

http://publishing.about.com/od/BookAuthorBasics/a/Writing-Good-Book-Titles-What-Makes-A-Good-Book-Title.htm

http://stemcell.stanford.edu/research/

http://thinkexist.com/quotation/happiness_is_the_meaning_and_the_purpose_of_life/171697.html - Aristotle quote

I Am documentary by Tom Shadyac

Lateral Thinking by Edward de Bono

Poetics by Aristotle

The First Breath by Crystal Enlightenment

REFERENCES CONTINUED

The First Five Pages by Noah Lukeman

The Problem Isn't Piracy. The Problem Is Obscurity. By Cory Doctorow, compiled by Children's Book Insider

Visions of the Ascended Masters by Kinsley Jarrett

Wealth Seminar by Dymphna Boholt

Wikipedia

www.allenandunwin.com.au

www.artslaw.com.au/info-sheets/info-sheet/exclusion-clauses-disclaimers-and-risk-warnings/#headingh36

www.collinsdictionary.com/dictionary/english/

www.digitalbookworld.com/2014/2014-author-survey-indie-authors-and-others-prefer-traditional-publishing-slightly/

www.easywaytowrite

www.health.com

www.ipaustralia.gov.au

www.lighttechnology.com/store/books/sanat-kumara-training-planetary-logos - *The Story of Sanat Kumara* by Janet McClure

www.matthaig.com/10-reasons-not-to-be-a-writer/

REFERENCES CONTINUED

www.penguin.com.au

www.thebookdesigner.com/2010/01/6-copyright-page-disclaimers-and-giving-credit/

www.thefreedictionary.com

www.theguardian.com/books/2014/jan/17/writ

www.urbandictionary.com/

www.wonderopolis.org

About the Author

Danae Andrea Harwood lives in Black Rock, eighteen kilometres south east of Melbourne's central business district, Victoria, Australia. She enjoys Zumba and Body Combat.

Danae has a Bachelor of Arts degree from Victoria College with Story, Script, and Feature Article Writing as her majors. She has completed children's book writing courses with multi-published author Robyn Opie Parnell and Allen and Unwin's Faber Academy.

Writing has always been part of Danae's life. Danae became conscious of her connection to writing when her primary school teacher asked her to read to the class the sentences she'd written for spelling words. The teacher then encouraged the other children to put the spelling words into more meaningful, imaginative sentences. Danae's first published piece was a poem in a pop music magazine about male singer Marilyn.

Danae has written manuscripts for picture books, chapter books, middle grade readers, and YA novels. She has authored several published feature articles. Danae is undertaking the final edit of a YA novel that she aims to enter in the Amazon Breakthrough Novel Award Contest.

The info, insights, and affirmations Danae presents in *The Writer's Runway Volume 1* have helped Danae to stay on the aspiring writer's journey and pick up speed by providing her with a solid runway of knowledge and ongoing support.

If you wish to contact Danae, please visit her website at www.danae-andrea.com .

Disclaimer

The author is unable to guarantee professional writing success as a result of reading and applying this book's contents. The information in this book is intended to be used as a supplement only to the study of writing and marketing.

The author has made every effort to ensure that the collated, factual information is true and correct and comes from reliable sources. The personal insights and affirmations are the author's views only and serve merely as suggestions.

The author disclaims any liability of loss, damage, negligence, or disruption to any party directly or indirectly as a result of errors, omissions, inaccuracies, or actions taken on account of this book's contents. In the event that any statement in this book causes offence, this is unintentional.

The reader is to take the four references to Ascended Masters as strategies for creating a mindset conducive to writing, not as any promotion of spiritual ideology. The reader may substitute the insights that refer to Ascended Masters with his or her own insights that refer to masters or muses of choice such as another writer or a hero, alternative spiritual figures, the reader's higher self, an inspiring organisation, or anything created by the reader that represents inspiration, peace, and attainment.

If a reader finds any part of this book to be harmful, insensitive, in error, or reckless in any way, please email the author at soulsafari@hotmail.com .

The Reference section is a list of information sources only and excludes endorsement of the author by the sources and vice versa.

The author disclaims any liability that may arise on account of virus transmittal from visiting the websites/links listed in the Reference section of this book.

Notes